—•COOK•—

SERVE
UP JOY

— COOK —

SERVE UP JOY

recipes for sharing

THE COOK KITCHEN

K

Dedicated to the original cooks,
Dale and Liz, and all those who've
followed in their footsteps.

First published in Great Britain in 2025 by Kyle Books,
an imprint of Octopus Publishing Group Ltd
Carmelite House
50 Victoria Embankment
London EC4Y 0DZ
www.octopusbooks.co.uk
www.octopusbooksusa.com

An Hachette UK Company
www.hachette.co.uk

The authorised representative in the EEA is
Hachette Ireland, 8 Castlecourt Centre,
Castleknock Road, Castleknock, Dublin 15,
D15 YF6A, Ireland (email: info@hbgi.ie)

Text copyright © The COOK Kitchen 2025

Distributed in the US by Hachette Book Group,
1290 Avenue of the Americas, 4th and 5th Floors
New York, NY 10104

Distributed in Canada by Canadian Manda Group
664 Annette St., Toronto, Ontario, Canada M6S 2C8

ISBN 978-1-80419-292-4

A CIP catalogue record for this book is available
from the British Library.

Printed and bound in China.

10 9 8 7 6 5 4 3 2 1

Publisher: Joanna Copestick
Art Director: Jaz Bahra
Senior Editor: Leanne Bryan
Copy Editor: Sarah Reece
Photographer: Carolyn Barber
Food and Props Stylist: Libby Silbermann
Illustrator: Holly Wales
Senior Production Manager: Katherine Hockley

The COOK team
Brand Director and Head of Content: Claire Postans
Chief Creative Officer: James Rutter
Head of Brand Design: Hannah Goodacre

www.cookfood.net
@thecookkitchen
@thecookkitchen

In 2013, COOK became one of the UK's first
certified B Corps, committed to using our
business as a force for good.

MIX
Paper | Supporting
responsible forestry
FSC® C008047

CONTENTS

Cooking done with care is an act of love

Craig Claiborne

HELLO!

Here's one thing we know: nothing brings people together better than sharing a good meal.

This book is our attempt to condense the learnings and joy of growing COOK into a couple of hundred printed pages. We've gone from a ramshackle little kitchen in Rainham, Kent, making handmade frozen meals, sold from a tiny shop in Farnham, Surrey, to an award-winning, ethical business with four big kitchens and more than 100 shops nationwide.

If we were to reduce down the lessons from that journey into a flavour-packed, sticky, irresistible sauce, it would be this: care for each other.

Every day, we bring this idea to life by making and sharing good food, using the recipes you'll find inside this book. They're not the quickest to make ... but then creating deep, satisfying flavours can't be rushed. Putting in the time and effort most definitely pays off.

When we share a great meal, we forge a powerful human connection. We leave the table nourished in both body and soul. The more we eat together, the better it is for all of us.

We hope this book gives you the confidence to bring loved ones together around the table to enjoy a delicious home-cooked meal. As American food writer Craig Claiborne put it, 'Cooking done with care is an act of love.' And, yes, love makes the world go round.

So, whether it's family or friends, two of you or twenty, let's get cooking and serve up some joy!

All at COOK

WELCOME TO OUR TABLE

By Ed, James and Rosie, the siblings behind COOK

Food and family, cooking and community. These are what serving up joy is all about and what lives at the very heart of COOK.

Our story goes back to our family dinner table in the 1980s. To feed the six of us, Mum would batch cook a chilli or casserole and freeze the extra in ice-cream tubs, stacked in our chest freezer. When supper was needed in a hurry, she would pop a tub in the microwave and dinner would be sorted. What's more, the meal tasted just as good as when we ate it the first time around. The beauty of frozen food! To this day, everything we try to achieve at COOK is to replicate the quality of the home-cooked food Mum used to make. Thanks, Mum.

Mum and Dad also taught us the power of food to connect people. Fuelled by their strong faith, they would often invite vulnerable or lonely people over for a meal – not something we always appreciated as moody teenagers. But it taught us the value of community, and that our table should have room for everyone – principles we try to bring to life through COOK today.

They were also entrepreneurs, opening the first Italian-style coffee shops in the towns of Tonbridge and Sevenoaks in Kent in the 1980s, when nobody could even pronounce 'cappuccino'. Alongside fancy coffee, they sold cakes baked by Mum's best friend, Diana Maher. The cakes were so good they soon had other businesses asking if they could stock them. And so, with Diana, they opened a small bakery selling cakes wholesale. Frozen, of course – cakes freeze wonderfully!

Diana had one condition on joining the business. Having worked as a cook in a drug rehab centre, she wanted to offer jobs to people who'd been through treatment and were struggling to find work. The idea

of using business for social good was, literally, baked into the way the company worked. We were lucky to grow up believing this was simply how things should be – business used for good, not just for profit.

From these seeds, the idea for COOK began to take root in Ed's brain – frozen meals like Mum made, sold in shops of our own not the supermarkets, by a different kind of company. In 1996, after five years working for the family bakery, Ed went out on his own with a £30,000 loan and a brilliant chef, Dale Penfold, as his co-founder. They set up a production kitchen in a disused pizza-delivery site in Rainham, Kent and,

Previous page: (top) Dad and Mum, Andrew and Anne Perry, in the 1970s; (bottom) Our first shop, Cakes & Casseroles, Farnham, Surrey, 1997. This page: (above) Our launch; (right and far right) The original cooks – Liz Dove and Dale Penfold. Opposite page: James, Rosie and Ed.

in March 1997, they opened a tiny shop in Farnham, Surrey, called Cakes & Casseroles.

An overnight success it was not. Making frozen meals like Mum's at scale turned out to be much, much harder than Ed and Dale had imagined. But we sold enough to survive. Just. And gradually Dale figured out how to make the food taste really good. By the end of 1999, there was a second shop in Tunbridge Wells, Kent, opened by Matt Hills, a schoolfriend of Ed's. We'd also teamed up with Liz Dove, who was making incredible frozen puddings from her garage in suburban Surrey and would go on to set up the COOK Puddings kitchen in Somerset (see page 186).

While Ed was a great shopkeeper and Dale was a talented and resourceful chef, neither had a clue about running a business. They had no admin, no accounts, no stocktake and, they realized, no money. Luckily, they had Ed's brother James, who'd just started running the

family bakery. He suggested merging the two businesses to bring some desperately needed stability to Ed and Dale's chaotic start-up. Yes, please.

Ed and James came together to run the business, with Ed's wife Sophie taking charge of the brand and changing the name to COOK. Our sister Rosie joined a couple of years later, stepping up to run things with Ed in 2012, when James became Chair. Mixing family and business isn't always straightforward. We've all had to work hard at it, learning to let go of the occasional unintended pain, to hold tight to the shared sense of mission and, always, to remember it's better to be together than in agreement.

By the early 2000s, COOK was growing fast. Banks were happy to lend us lots of money and our parents bravely agreed to let us sell the bakery and coffee shops (their pension!) and pour everything into COOK. We weren't making any profit, but we had a big, shiny new kitchen and 30 shops.

Then, in 2008, the financial crisis hit. We came as close to going bust as is possible without actually going bust. But that near-death experience gave us a renewed sense of purpose and commitment to building a stable, successful business that genuinely makes a difference. And it's the journey we've been on ever since.

We believe business needs to change and, in 2013, this took us to the USA to meet the companies building a movement to use business as a force for good, as certified B Corporations. We discovered a vibrant community of inspiring companies and a framework for operating business for people and planet, not just profit. We certified COOK and, in 2015, James set about launching the movement in the UK. Today, the UK has approaching 3,000 B Corps, the most of any nation outside the USA. All have the duty to create value for everyone – team, communities, planet – alongside profit for shareholders.

At COOK, we express this in many ways: through our commitment to being one of the country's best companies to work for; through our RAW Talent programme helping people into sustainable work after prison, homelessness, long-term unemployment or mental ill health; through our Community Kitchen, bringing together people in need over a shared meal; and through our work with farmers and campaigners to change our food system for the better.

At the heart of it all, there is always food and family, cooking and community. COOK has always been about nourishing relationships: with each other, our customers and communities. To all those who've contributed over the years, our heartfelt thanks. Whatever success we have enjoyed is down to you.

FROM OUR KITCHENS TO YOURS

'I've fallen for a chef called Wayne,' read the headline in the *Observer Food Monthly* back in the early 2000s, when journalist Mimi Spencer discovered just how good our meals were. Why Wayne? Because printed proudly on the front label of every COOK meal you'll find the name and signature of the chef who made it. Cynical folk assume this is a marketing ruse. But our chefs are the real deal (the Wayne in question now runs one of our kitchens in Kent).

Every day, our chefs are cooking on a grand scale, often making 1,500 portions of a recipe at a time. They'll soften onions, brown the meat, thicken the sauce and stir in herbs, just as you would at home. Only, they'll be using a giant, steam-heated pan; kilos of butter and flour; and a big paddle rather than a wooden spoon. They sign off each batch they make, so their name can go on the label.

As they'll tell you, the way we cook isn't for people in a rush. We marinate for hours; we braise slowly; we simmer until the flavours are deep and rich. We believe great taste takes time and care. At our daily taste panel meetings, we sample a portion of every batch cooked the day before. If it doesn't look and taste exactly right, we'll sell it at a discounted price as a Chef's Mistake.

Most of the recipes in this book are simply scaled-down versions of what our chefs make in our kitchens. They're dishes we've been cooking for years, for which people come back again and again. Many have won Great Taste awards. Basically, they're guaranteed winners.

We've tweaked some of the recipes a bit to work better in a home kitchen, and we've reinvented a few completely. We've also raided our archive for dishes

we no longer make for one reason or another. And in the Salads and Sides chapter we've included a handful of our favourite salad recipes (frozen salads being a bit weird ... which isn't to say we haven't tried). Finally, at the bottom of many recipes, we've included our chefs' serving tips and suggestions: finishing touches that make all the difference.

We also asked our chefs for their home kitchen tips. Top of the list is to make sure you have good-quality, sharp knives. Over the years, we've realized professional cooks tend to be mildly obsessive about knives – sharpening them, in particular. George, who heads our development kitchen, concedes it's true. His home kitchen has dozens of knives displayed proudly on the wall on magnetic strips, but he suggests you can get by with just four: a chef's knife for general chopping; a paring knife for more delicate tasks; a carving knife; and a bread knife. Invest as much as you can on these four knives, look after them, and they'll last you a lifetime of cookery.

Jamie, our executive chef, says that when it comes to sharpness, there are two cardinal sins to avoid: keeping knives in a drawer with other utensils and cleaning them in a dishwasher. Both will take the edge off. For storage, have a magnetic strip on the wall or a knife block. And to clean them, just take a few seconds to wipe the blades carefully.

To sharpen blades, invest in a steel or a whetstone, watch some YouTube videos, and then sharpen little and often (ideally before each use). Alternatively, George recommends a little sharpening gadget called an AnySharp, which is inexpensive and foolproof.

Once your knives are sorted, you're ready to chop like a pro. For guidance, we turned to Robin, who for more than a decade was in charge of our Prep Kitchen, where all the peeling, chopping, slicing and dicing happens (he's since taken over our Pastry team). Robin says the secret to chopping is to learn 'the claw' – follow our illustrated guide on the right.

Chop Like a Pro

1 Make a claw with your non-chopping hand (pretend you're a bear!).

2 Put your claw on the chopping board – your knuckles should extend beyond your fingertips.

3 Use your knuckles to guide the knife blade, keeping the tip of the knife on the board. Chop, slowly moving your claw along the ingredient you're chopping.

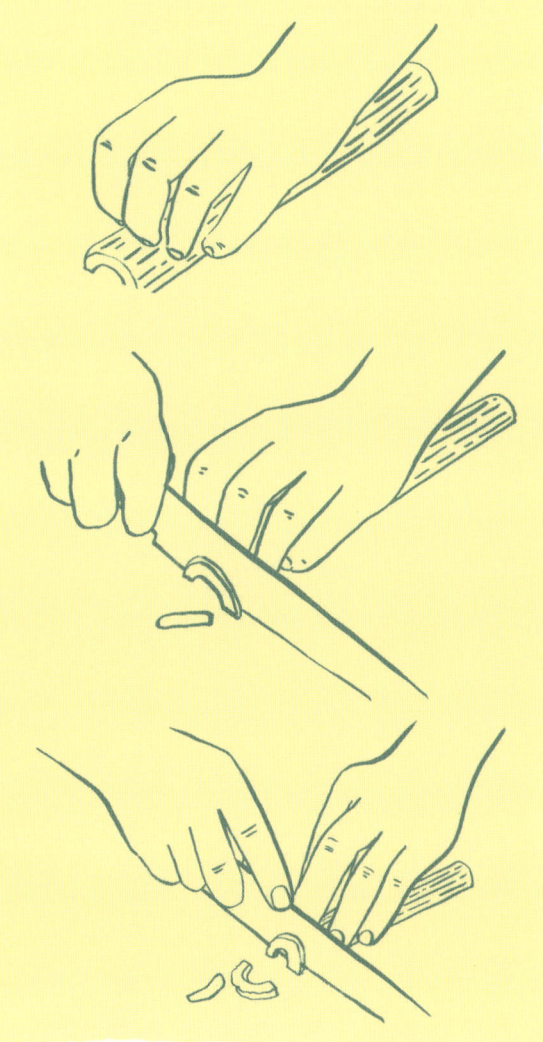

With your knives and chopping skills taken care of, what about more esoteric kitchen kit? We asked our chefs for the less common utensils that they think everybody should have in their cupboards. Here are a few to try:

Silpat mat ... a reusable, nonstick mat for baking (bye-bye greaseproof paper). Creates a lovely crisp bottom on your bake, and rolls up nice and small. *Jo, development chef*

Dough scraper ... not just for dough! It's great for transferring chopped veg from chopping board to pan. Also, fab for cleaning up any mess. *George, development chef*

Microplane grater ... for grating anything finely (garlic, ginger, lemon zest) – and it makes Parmesan go so much further. *Tony, chef*

Potato ricer ... the secret to silky smooth mashed potato. *Darren, chef*

Temperature probe ... why wouldn't you want to get the temperature of meat or fish spot on? *Channaporn, chef*

Mandoline ... saves so much time fine-slicing veg, especially for Dauphinoise Potatoes (see page 183) – but mind your fingers! *Chris, chef*

Mezzaluna knife ... a curved, double-handled knife that makes fine-chopping herbs a breeze. *Louis, chef*

Blow torch ... you'll be surprised how often you use it. *Lewis, chef*

We'd love to know how you get on with your chopping, your utensils and, of course, your cooking. Drop us a line and let us know which recipes you try and any little twists or variations you come up with (email ServeUpJoy@cookfood.net or share on our socials, @thecookkitchen).

From all our chefs and kitchen teams, we wish you the very best in serving up joy.

The GOATs

Keep an eye out for the goat symbol on some of our recipes – this stands for the Greatest Of All Time. Remarkably, seven of the savoury dishes we cooked when we opened our first shop back in 1997 remain on our menu today, the recipes little changed, as do three puddings we first started selling in 1999. The greatest of all time, indeed.

It seems that, when it comes to the comforting flavours of home, our tastes really don't change so much. We want something hearty and filling. Uncomplicated but not basic. And it seems cheese helps, too. Which, come to think of it, is a pretty good motto for life. Suffice to say, if you have a few of these recipes in your kitchen repertoire, you'll never be short of people eager for a seat at your table.

Chicken Alexander (see page 18)

Macaroni Cheese (see page 35)

Chicken, Ham and Leek Pie
(see page 48)

Vegetable Lasagne (see page 60)

Classic Fish Pie (see page 70)

Beef Bourguignon (see page 84)

Coq au Vin (see page 100)

Raspberry Pavlova (see page 191)

Chocolate and Raspberry Roulade
(see page 192)

Classic Lemon Cheesecake
(see pages 195–6)

Batch and Freeze

Batch cooking for the freezer is our specialist subject. When you see this little logo next to a recipe, it means it's perfect for batch cooking and freezing. In other words, you can cook larger quantities – more than you need for tonight's dinner – and then freeze the extra so you've got a time-saving supper for another day. Batch cooking really isn't rocket science. It just needs a little bit of forethought.

– Make sure there's space in the freezer.

– Have pans big enough to cook larger quantities.

– Check you've got good-quality reusable plastic or glass containers. Freezer bags are great for sauces – freezing them flat also helps with space, as you can stack them on top of each other.

– Allow food to cool before freezing.

– Label, label, label ... avoid UFOs (Unidentified Frozen Objects). Always write the name, date and number of portions on the bag or container before you freeze.

'An apron is just a
cape on backwards'

– Anon

KITCHEN WISDOM NO.1

Weekday
Wonders

Let's face it, serving up joy
on a cold, wet Tuesday in
February can be a big ask.

Herein lies the answer:
simple dishes to savour.

Chicken Alexander

PREP: 10 MINUTES · COOK: 30–40 MINUTES · SERVES 4

2 tablespoons rapeseed oil

2–3 chicken breasts, total weight
   400g (14oz), diced

30g (1oz) unsalted butter

1 onion, finely sliced

½ red pepper, cored, deseeded
   and finely sliced

½ yellow pepper, cored, deseeded
   and finely sliced

100g (3½oz) chestnut mushrooms,
   trimmed and finely sliced

30ml (2 tablespoons) sherry

100ml (3½fl oz) dry white wine

300ml (10fl oz) good chicken stock

1 tablespoon cornflour

150ml (5fl oz) double cream

2 tablespoons lemon juice

salt and pepper

TO SERVE

1 tablespoon chopped flat leaf parsley

2 tablespoons chopped chives

grated Parmesan cheese

*Pretty much anything goes with this.
Try rice or potatoes with something
vibrant and green, like steamed,
buttered sugar snap peas. Or stir
through some cooked pappardelle
or linguine pasta (mix in a splash
of the pasta water for a really silky
sauce), garnish with pea shoots or
salad leaves, and sprinkle with extra
grated Parmesan.*

Chicken in a silky, cream and wine sauce with sweet peppers, mushrooms and fresh herbs. Back in 1997, when Dale created our first menu, he insisted on including Chicken à la King – a 1970s dinner-party staple. But it was the era of Cool Britannia and no one wanted reminding of just how uncool Britain had been in the 1970s. It flopped. The recipe, however, was too good to let go, so we gave it a new name – one of Dale's middle names, in fact – and Chicken Alexander was born. We're saving Dale's other middle name, Colchester, for a real emergency. If you're going to batch and freeze, leave out the lemon juice, herbs and Parmesan and add them after reheating.

Heat the oil in a large nonstick frying pan on a medium–high heat. Once hot, add the diced chicken, season, then brown on all sides until lightly golden – this will take about 5 minutes. Remove the chicken from the pan and place in a bowl to one side.

In the same frying pan, melt the butter, then add the onion and fry on a medium heat for 5–10 minutes until translucent. Add the peppers and mushrooms and fry for a further 5–10 minutes or until the mushrooms are turning golden.

Add the sherry and white wine and cook until reduced by half. Add the chicken stock. Place the cornflour in a small bowl and, using a spoon, mix in a little of the cooking liquid to make a paste. Add the paste to the pan and cook for a further 5 minutes, or until the sauce has slightly thickened.

Return the chicken to the pan, reduce the heat to medium–low, bring to a simmer, then cook for 5 minutes, stirring regularly, until the chicken is cooked through. Stir in the double cream and heat through for a couple of minutes. Season to taste and stir in the lemon juice.

Scatter over the chopped herbs and a little grated Parmesan, then serve.

Broccoli and Spinach Pesto Chicken

PREP: 10 MINUTES · COOK: 50 MINUTES · SERVES 4–6

½ head broccoli

2 tablespoons unsalted butter

200g (7oz) baby spinach

100ml (3½fl oz) milk

200ml (7fl oz) double cream

4 tablespoons basil pesto

50g (1¾oz) Parmesan cheese, grated

1 lemon

4 chicken breasts, 175–200g (6–7oz) each, skin on

2 tablespoons rapeseed oil

few fresh oregano sprigs or
1 teaspoon dried oregano

250g (9oz) cherry tomatoes

1 × 125g (4½oz) ball mozzarella cheese

salt and pepper

Roasted new potatoes are perfect on the side – parboil, then roast on the shelf below the chicken. Or try pasta (we like pappardelle) – remove the chicken breasts once cooked, stir the sauce through the cooked pasta, then slice the chicken and arrange on top. The sauce is also great with salmon fillets or on its own with pasta. You can use sun-dried tomato or red pepper pesto instead of basil, too.

Transform a common jar of pesto into something a little bit special. This is based on our Pesto, Broccoli and Spinach frozen sauce, the brainchild of Matt in our commercial team, who opened our second-ever store in Tunbridge Wells in 1998. For years he's been saying we should make frozen sauces that you can use in lots of different ways. Finally, we gave in to his badgering. And, it turns out, frozen sauces are a pretty good idea.

Start by making the sauce. Trim the broccoli into small florets and place in a food processor. Blitz to tiny, rice-sized pieces, then tip into a large microwave-proof bowl. Add 2 tablespoons of water and cook in a microwave on full power for 3 minutes, or until cooked through. Alternatively, cook in a little boiling water in a small saucepan on the hob for 1–2 minutes. Drain and fluff up with a fork and place to one side.

Place a large frying pan on a medium heat and add the butter. Allow the butter to melt, then add the spinach. Place a lid on the pan, or cover with tin foil, and allow the spinach to wilt. As soon as it's wilted, use a slotted spoon to scoop the spinach out into a clean tea towel. When cool enough to handle, squeeze out the excess water or press through a colander. Turn the spinach out onto a chopping board and chop finely. Alternatively, you can pulse briefly in the food processor (you want it to retain some texture). Stir the spinach into the broccoli and season.

Heat the milk and cream in a saucepan on a low heat until just steaming. Stir in the pesto, then the Parmesan. Allow the cheese to melt, then stir in the chopped broccoli and spinach. Cook for 2–3 minutes. Season to taste and add a good squeeze of lemon juice. Stir once more, pour into a medium roasting tray and place to one side.

Preheat the oven to 180°C fan/200°C/400°F/Gas Mark 6.

Season the chicken breasts all over and drizzle with the oil. Place a large frying pan on a medium heat, brown the chicken breasts on both sides, then place in the roasting tray on top of the sauce. Scatter over the oregano and dot the cherry tomatoes around. Tear the mozzarella into pieces and arrange on top of the chicken. Bake in the oven for 30 minutes until the chicken is golden and cooked through.

Chicken Tikka Skewers with Lime and Coriander Rice

PREP: 25 MINUTES, PLUS MARINATING (AND SOAKING SKEWERS, IF USING BAMBOO) ·
COOK: 25 MINUTES · SERVES 4–6

FOR THE MARINATED CHICKEN

4 garlic cloves, crushed

3 tablespoons tomato purée

2 tablespoons rapeseed oil

150ml (5fl oz) natural yoghurt

2 teaspoons ground coriander

2 teaspoons ground cumin

2 teaspoons garam masala

2 teaspoons smoked paprika

½ teaspoon chilli flakes

1 thumb-sized piece of ginger,
    peeled and grated

50g (1¾oz) fresh coriander, chopped

600g (1lb 5oz) chicken thighs or
    breasts, cut into chunks

salt and pepper

lemon wedges, to serve

FOR THE LIME AND CORIANDER RICE

200g (7oz) basmati rice or wild rice

1 lime

10g (¼oz) fresh coriander, chopped

salt and pepper

FOR THE RAITA

¼ cucumber, halved and deseeded

1 small garlic clove, crushed

150ml (5fl oz) natural yoghurt

10g (¼oz) mint leaves, chopped

You can also make a quick, fresh chutney by dicing ¼ red onion and a handful of cherry tomatoes. Mix together with a squeeze of lime juice and seasoning.

Our cheat's chicken tikka, based on a one-pot recipe we used to make. The longer you can marinate, the better, but needs must ... just give it as long as you can. We'd always pick chicken thighs over breasts for this. They are not only cheaper but more succulent. You'll need eight skewers – you can use bamboo or metal ones. If you're using bamboo, these will need to be soaked in water for 1 hour before you start cooking the chicken. Don't forget the poppadums and mango chutney – who wouldn't want them on the side?

Start by marinating the chicken. Place all the marinade ingredients in a large bowl or container, reserving a little of the fresh coriander to garnish, and stir well. Add the chicken along with a good pinch of salt and pepper. Toss to combine, cover and place in the fridge for as long as you can.

Preheat the grill to medium. Thread the chicken pieces onto the skewers and arrange on an oven tray. Place the chicken under the grill and cook for 10–12 minutes, turning the skewers every few minutes to ensure even cooking. Cook until the chicken is tender and the juices run clear. Remove from under the grill and place to one side under a layer of tin foil.

Meanwhile, make the lime and coriander rice. Add the rice to a small saucepan. Pour over enough boiling water to ensure there is 2 parts water to 1 part rice. Bring to the boil, then reduce to a simmer and cook according to the packet instructions. When the water has all been absorbed, remove from the heat. Fluff the rice with a fork and allow to stand for 2 minutes. Season to taste, then add a good squeeze of lime juice and stir through the coriander.

Meanwhile, make the raita. Coarsely grate the cucumber into a bowl and add the garlic and a pinch of salt. Stir in the yoghurt and chopped mint, reserving a little mint to garnish. Check the seasoning.

Scatter the reserved coriander and mint leaves over the rice and serve with the chicken skewers on top and the raita on the side. Serve with lemon wedges for squeezing over.

Moroccan-spiced Harissa Chicken

PREP: 15 MINUTES · COOK: 55 MINUTES · SERVES 4

6 boneless, skinless chicken thighs, total weight about 680g (1lb 8oz), sliced

2 aubergines, chopped into chunks

1 × 400g (14oz) can chickpeas, drained

2 teaspoons ground ginger

2 teaspoons ground cinnamon

2 teaspoons ground turmeric

2 tablespoons ground cumin

4 tablespoons rapeseed oil

3–4 tablespoons mild rose or apricot harissa paste

2 onions, chopped

3 garlic cloves, chopped

30g (1oz) fresh coriander, leaves picked and stalks chopped

1 teaspoon cayenne pepper

2 tablespoons tomato purée

1 × 400g (14oz) can chopped tomatoes

400ml (14fl oz) chicken stock

salt and pepper

20g (¾oz) flaked almonds, toasted, to garnish

We've tweaked our award-winning recipe for a home kitchen and, to be honest, we think this version might be better! We first made this in the pre-internet era. Jamie, our young development chef (still with us, less young), spent a day at the library poring over cookbooks to find the right spice mix. We went through a phase of adding orange juice to the sauce which, in hindsight, was a bit weird. Serve with fruity couscous (see tip, below), rice, pitta bread or flatbreads (see page 36).

Preheat the oven to 180°C fan/200°C/400°F/Gas Mark 6. Line a large roasting tray with nonstick baking paper.

Place the chicken in the prepared tray, then add the aubergines and chickpeas. Add half of the ground spices, 3 tablespoons of the oil and 3 tablespoons of the harissa paste. Give everything a good stir. Season, then bake in the oven for 40 minutes, turning the contents of the tray halfway through the cooking time.

Meanwhile, make the sauce. Place a large, shallow casserole pan on a medium heat. Add the remaining oil, onions, garlic and coriander stalks. Cook for 10 minutes, stirring occasionally, until the onions are cooked and starting to colour. Add the cayenne pepper, tomato purée and the remaining spices and harissa paste. Cook for a further 2 minutes. Add the chopped tomatoes and chicken stock. Bring to the boil, then reduce the heat and simmer for 30 minutes, stirring occasionally.

When the chicken and vegetables are cooked through, remove the tray from the oven and carefully tip the contents into the pan with the sauce. Stir well. Simmer for a further 10 minutes, then season to taste. You can add a splash of water at this stage if the sauce is a bit thick.

Sprinkle the toasted almonds and coriander leaves over the chicken, then serve with your chosen side.

Couscous is our go-to side. To ensure yours isn't bland or boring, make it with chicken or vegetable stock rather than water, add some turmeric for colour, a squeeze of lemon for flavour and some dried cranberries or sultanas for sweetness. Just before you serve, stir through some chopped mint or parsley and maybe some diced tomatoes or cucumber.

Chicken and Tomato Pasta Bake

PREP: 25 MINUTES · COOK: 1 HOUR · SERVES 4–6

4 tablespoons rapeseed oil,
    plus extra for greasing
1 onion, finely diced
2 garlic cloves, crushed
30g (1oz) basil, leaves picked and
    chopped, and stalks chopped,
    plus extra to garnish (optional)
½ tablespoon dried oregano
2 × 400g (14oz) cans chopped
    tomatoes
250ml (9fl oz) chicken stock
20g (¾oz) unsalted butter
2 chicken breasts, skinless, about
    150g (5½oz) each, sliced
200g (7oz) chestnut mushrooms,
    trimmed and sliced
280g (10oz) dried pasta
85g (3oz) breadcrumbs
2 tablespoons red pesto
1 × 125g (4½oz) ball mozzarella, sliced
salt and pepper

There are times when a great-tasting, hearty bowl of no-frills food is just what you need. This is it with bells on – which is why the recipe hasn't changed in 25 years. It's a great way to use up leftover roast chicken, too – just add it to the sauce before mixing in the pasta.

Start by making the sauce. Place half of the oil in a large, shallow, ovenproof casserole pan and place on a medium heat. Add the onion, garlic, basil stalks and oregano. Cook for about 10 minutes, or until the onions are translucent, stirring well to stop the ingredients catching. Add the chopped tomatoes and stock. Bring to the boil, reduce the heat and allow to simmer for about 20 minutes. The sauce will be fairly thin at this stage but don't worry, the chicken and pasta will soak up the sauce.

Meanwhile, place a large frying pan on a medium heat. Add the remaining oil and the butter. When the butter has melted, add the chicken and mushrooms. Cook for 10 minutes, stirring occasionally, until the chicken is cooked through and golden. Season, then add the chicken and mushrooms to the casserole pan containing the sauce.

Preheat the oven to 200°C fan/220°C/425°F/Gas Mark 7.

Place a large pan of salted water on to boil and cook the pasta according to the packet instructions until al dente. Drain, saving a cup of the pasta water to add to the sauce.

Meanwhile, mix the breadcrumbs, pesto and chopped basil leaves in a bowl to make the topping.

Tip the cooked pasta into the casserole pan along with the reserved pasta water. Toss the pasta and sauce together to combine. Arrange the mozzarella slices on top. Sprinkle over the topping and bake in the oven for 10 minutes, or until the top is golden and the sauce bubbling. Remove from the oven and allow to sit for 5 minutes before serving, garnished with basil leaves, if liked.

A lightly dressed green salad is all you need on the side.

King Prawn Linguine

PREP: 10 MINUTES · COOK: 40 MINUTES · SERVES 4

4 anchovy fillets, in oil

1 tablespoon olive oil

1 onion, finely chopped

3 garlic cloves, finely chopped

10g (¼oz) flat leaf parsley, leaves picked and chopped, stalks finely chopped

2 teaspoons crushed fennel seeds

1 teaspoon chilli flakes

½ teaspoon ground turmeric

150ml (5fl oz) white wine

400ml (14fl oz) fish stock

1 × 400g (14oz) can chopped tomatoes

60g (2¼oz) roasted red peppers in oil, chopped

60g (2¼oz) semi-dried tomatoes in oil, chopped

300g (10½oz) dried linguine

300g (10½oz) raw king prawns

1 lemon, cut into wedges

salt and pepper

This is a pretty sophisticated dish for a weeknight but, hey, we're classy people (sometimes). It's all about the layers of flavour in the sauce. It never fails to give us a little taste of Mediterranean sunshine, even on a gloomy, wet Wednesday in November. Serve with some crusty bread and a green salad.

Place a large frying pan on a medium heat and add the anchovy fillets, along with 1 tablespoon of their oil. Fry for a few minutes, or until the fillets break down. Add the olive oil, followed by the onion, garlic and parsley stalks. Fry for 5 minutes, or until the onions are cooked but translucent. Add the fennel seeds, chilli flakes and turmeric and cook for a further 30 seconds. Add the white wine and simmer, allowing the wine to reduce by half. Add the fish stock, chopped tomatoes, roasted red peppers and semi-dried tomatoes. Simmer, uncovered, for 20 minutes.

Meanwhile, place a large pan of salted water on to boil. When you're nearly ready to serve, cook the pasta according to the packet instructions. Drain, saving a cup of the pasta water to add to the sauce.

Add the prawns to the sauce with a squeeze of lemon juice. Cook for about 5 minutes, or until they turn pink. Season to taste.

Add the pasta, the reserved pasta water and the parsley leaves to the sauce, and toss with the prawns.

Divide between plates and serve with lemon wedges.

To make your linguine look fancy on the plate, it's all about the twirl! You'll need a big dinner fork, carving fork or kitchen tongs, and a serving spoon. When everything's mixed together, pick up a decent amount of pasta with the fork or tongs and twirl it around on the spoon so it wraps around the fork or tongs. Carefully slide the twirled pasta into the middle of a plate. Arrange the prawns artfully on top, garnish with extra chopped parsley or maybe a few rocket leaves, and serve with a lemon wedge on the side.

Warm Prawn Noodle Salad with Mango and Green Bean Salsa

PREP: 20 MINUTES · COOK: 15 MINUTES · SERVES 4

FOR THE SALSA

100g (3½oz) fine green beans, trimmed and sliced into 3cm (1¼ inch) pieces

1 red pepper, cored, deseeded and finely chopped

3 spring onions, trimmed and finely sliced

1 ripe mango, cut into small cubes

4 tablespoons toasted sesame oil

1 lime

FOR THE SALAD

200g (7oz) wholemeal noodle nests

1 tablespoon rapeseed oil

20g (¾oz) piece of fresh root ginger, peeled and grated

2 garlic cloves, crushed

2 red chillies, deseeded and sliced

3 spring onions, trimmed and finely sliced

200g (7oz) raw king prawns

100g (3½oz) fresh or frozen garden peas

3 tablespoons fish sauce

1 carrot, peeled and cut into fine matchsticks

½ cucumber, deseeded and cut into fine matchsticks

2 tablespoons soy sauce

TO SERVE

small handful of fresh coriander

1 lime, cut into wedges

Zingy Asian flavours to brighten up a dreary weeknight. This offers the perfect solution for what to do with the mango you bought on a whim at the supermarket that's slowly going soft in the bottom of the fridge. Don't skimp on the chilli – the heat balances the sweet, fresh salsa perfectly.

First, make the salsa. Put a small saucepan of water on to boil and blanch the green beans for 2 minutes. Drain, run under cold water and place in a bowl. Add the red pepper, spring onions and mango. Add the sesame oil and the lime juice. Mix and place to one side.

Cook the noodles according to the packet instructions. Cool under running water, drain and place in a large mixing bowl.

Place a large frying pan on a high heat. Add the oil, ginger, garlic, chillies and spring onions, and stir-fry for 1 minute. Add the prawns, turn the heat down to medium and stir-fry for a further 2 minutes. Add the peas and fish sauce, and stir-fry until the peas and prawns are cooked through. Make sure the prawns have all turned pink and there are no grey bits remaining. Don't cook them for too long, though, or the flesh will become tough. Tip the prawns into the bowl with the noodles along with the carrot, cucumber and soy sauce. Toss to combine.

Transfer the noodle salad to a serving platter or individual plates. Spoon the salsa on top of the noodles. Scatter the coriander on top and serve with the lime wedges.

Use tongs or two forks to pile the noodles and prawns in the centre of four bowls. Spoon the salsa on top, nice and high. Sprinkle on the coriander leaves and add a bowl of prawn crackers on the side to share.

Macaroni Cheese

PREP: 10 MINUTES · COOK: 30 MINUTES · SERVES 4

40g (1½oz) unsalted butter,
    plus extra for greasing

568ml (1 pint) milk

2 bay leaves

6 black peppercorns

2 garlic cloves, crushed

40g (1½oz) plain flour

½ teaspoon paprika

200g (7oz) vintage or extra-mature
    Cheddar cheese, grated

50g (1¾oz) Parmesan cheese, grated

2 teaspoons English mustard

350g (12oz) dried pasta

40g (1½oz) fresh breadcrumbs

2 tablespoons chopped flat leaf parsley

1 teaspoon olive oil

salt and pepper

fresh thyme sprigs, to garnish (optional)

Mix it up by adding your own flavour flourishes. Try adding fried bacon lardons to the sauce for a salty kick, mix in roasted squash or cauliflower or broccoli florets before you grill, or experiment with different cheeses – Stilton for boldness or goats' cheese or feta for a lighter, more summery sauce.

The finest comfort food, bar none. Rich, cheesy and irresistible. Ours is quite a high-end recipe and the little touches we add in our kitchen make all the difference – the mustard, in particular, is a real winner. It's best eaten with steamed greens or a crunchy green salad. If you're cooking from frozen, cover with tin foil and cook for 50 minutes at 170°C fan/190°C/375°F/ Gas Mark 5, then remove the foil and cook for a further 10 minutes until the topping is golden.

Grease a 25 × 20cm (10 × 8 inch) ovenproof dish with butter.

Pour the milk into a saucepan, add the bay leaves and peppercorns, and place on a low heat for about 2 minutes. Make sure the milk doesn't boil – you just want the flavours to infuse the milk.

Place a medium saucepan on a low heat, then add the butter. When it's melted, add the garlic and stir continuously for 1 minute, allowing the garlic to cook but not colour. Stir in the flour and paprika. Cook, still stirring, for 2 minutes, or until the paste is golden and bubbling. Extract the bay leaves and peppercorns from the milk. Using a ladle, gradually add the milk, whisking between each addition to form a smooth sauce. Add most of the Cheddar and Parmesan, reserving 2 tablespoons of cheese for the topping, and stir in along with the mustard. Turn off the heat and place the sauce to one side.

Meanwhile, put a large saucepan of salted water on to boil and preheat the grill to high. Cook the pasta according to the packet instructions, but undercook it by 2 minutes. Drain, saving a cup of the pasta water to add to the sauce.

Meanwhile, mix the breadcrumbs and parsley in a bowl with the olive oil and a pinch each of salt and pepper. Add the reserved cheese and toss together.

Tip the slightly undercooked pasta into the sauce along with the reserved pasta water and stir to combine. Spoon the macaroni cheese into the prepared dish and sprinkle over the breadcrumb topping. It may look a little saucy at this point but the pasta will continue to cook and absorb the sauce. Keeping an eye on the dish throughout, place the dish under the grill for 10 minutes, or until golden and bubbling. Serve garnished with fresh thyme sprigs, if liked.

Shakshuka

PREP: 20 MINUTES · COOK: 1 HOUR · SERVES 4

FOR THE ROASTED VEGETABLES

1 large aubergine, chopped into
    large chunks

1 red pepper, cored, deseeded
    and sliced

1 green pepper, cored, deseeded
    and sliced

½ cauliflower (about 280g/10oz),
    separated into florets

6 tablespoons rapeseed oil

2 teaspoons cumin seeds

1 teaspoon caraway seeds

½ teaspoon chilli flakes

1 teaspoon ground cinnamon

½ teaspoon ground allspice

salt and pepper

FOR THE SAUCE

2 onions, finely chopped

3 garlic cloves, finely chopped

10g (¼oz) flat leaf parsley, leaves picked
    and stalks finely chopped

10g (¼oz) fresh coriander, leaves picked
    and stalks finely chopped

2 teaspoons ground cumin

1 teaspoon sweet smoked paprika

½ teaspoon chilli flakes

1 × 400g (14oz) can chickpeas, drained

2 × 400g (14oz) cans chopped tomatoes

6 dried apricots, chopped

4 eggs

FOR THE FLATBREADS

200g (7oz) self-raising flour,
    plus extra for dusting

200ml (7fl oz) natural yoghurt

pinch of ground cumin

pinch of sea salt

This Middle Eastern classic is a bit of a wonder dish, packed with veg, protein and big flavours. It's one of those recipes where anything goes – take the outline and make it your own. Definitely make extra to freeze, if you can. Reheat what you need from frozen in the microwave, then transfer to a pan to cook the eggs – it makes a truly epic weekend brunch served with our flatbreads.

Preheat the oven to 180°C fan/200°C/400°F/Gas Mark 6.

To make the roasted vegetables, place the aubergine, peppers and cauliflower in a large roasting tray lined with nonstick baking paper. Drizzle with 4 tablespoons of the oil and add all the spices. Season, then toss to combine. Roast in the oven for about 30 minutes, tossing the vegetables halfway through, until they are tender and golden.

Meanwhile, make the sauce. Place a large ovenproof frying pan or wide, shallow casserole pan on a medium heat. Add the remaining oil to the pan, along with the onions, garlic and parsley and coriander stalks. Fry for about 5 minutes, or until the onion is translucent. Add the spices and cook for 2 minutes. Add the chickpeas and cook for a further 5 minutes, stirring, until they are well coated in the spice mix and starting to dry out a little.

Add the tomatoes, then fill one of the cans with water and add that to the pan as well. Add the apricots, bring the sauce to the boil, then reduce to a simmer. Season, then allow the sauce to reduce for about 20 minutes, stirring occasionally.

When the roasted vegetables are cooked, carefully fold them into the sauce and allow to bubble for a further 10 minutes.

To make the flatbreads, mix the flour, yoghurt, cumin and salt together by hand in a large mixing bowl to form a dough. Cover and leave to rest for 15 minutes.

Divide the rested dough into four evenly sized pieces. On a lightly floured surface, roll out each piece of dough into a disc about 1.5cm (⅝ inch) thick. Heat a frying pan until hot and cook each disc for about 1 minute on each side until golden.

Next, make four wells in the shakshuka sauce and crack the eggs into them. Now you can either place the pan back in the oven to allow the eggs to set or keep the pan on the hob, cover with a lid and allow the eggs to steam on a medium–low heat for 10–15 minutes, or until cooked to your liking.

Scatter the parsley and coriander over the shakshuka and serve with flatbreads.

Halloumi with Pesto and Roasted Veg

PREP: 20 MINUTES · COOK: 45–50 MINUTES · SERVES 4

85g (3oz) walnut pieces or pine nuts

90g (3¼oz) mint, leaves picked

30g (1oz) flat leaf parsley, leaves picked

1 garlic clove

150ml (5fl oz) olive oil

juice of 1 lemon

1 × 250g (9oz) block halloumi cheese,
    sliced into 8 pieces

2 red peppers, cored, deseeded
    and sliced

2 yellow peppers, cored, deseeded
    and sliced

2 red onions, cut into wedges

3 tablespoons balsamic vinegar

1 tablespoon demerara sugar

salt and pepper

Penne pasta is invariably what we dig out from the cupboard to serve with this. Once cooked, you can add the pasta to the roasting tray (rather than the other way round) and give it all a good stir to make the most of the flavours. You can do the same with quinoa or any other grain, or parboil some new potatoes and roast them with the veg, or serve the halloumi and roasted veg with wraps and salad.

A no-fuss traybake that's great for meat-free Mondays (or any other day, come to that). We've suggested making the pesto from scratch but you could use a jar of good-quality shop-bought pesto instead. Swap in whatever veg you have in your fridge that roasts well – the balsamic glaze will add a gorgeous sweetness.

Preheat the oven to 180°C fan/200°C/400°F/Gas Mark 6.

Place a small frying pan on a medium heat. Add the nuts and toast for a few minutes, stirring regularly, until golden. Tip them onto a plate and allow to cool.

Meanwhile, make the pesto. Place the mint and parsley (reserving a few leaves of each to garnish) and the garlic into a food processor. Pulse a few times to roughly chop the leaves. Add the toasted nuts and pulse again. Add 100ml (3½fl oz) of the olive oil, the lemon juice and a splash of water. Pulse again to combine, season to taste, then scrape into a shallow bowl. Add the halloumi slices to the bowl and brush the pesto over them.

Meanwhile, place the peppers in a large roasting tray with the onions. Add the remaining 50ml (2fl oz) olive oil, the balsamic vinegar and sugar. Season and toss to coat. Roast in the oven for 10–15 minutes.

After this time, add the marinated halloumi to the oven tray – keep any leftover pesto in the bowl. Return the tray to the oven for about 25 minutes, or until the vegetables are cooked and the halloumi is golden.

Remove the tray from the oven, scatter over the reserved mint and parsley and any remaining pesto. Mix well, divide between bowls and dig in!

Roasted Cauliflower and Aubergine Dhal

PREP: 15 MINUTES · COOK: 45–55 MINUTES · SERVES 4–6

½ cauliflower, separated into florets

1 aubergine, chopped into chunks

5 tablespoons rapeseed oil

4 teaspoons garam masala

1 onion, finely diced

3 garlic cloves, crushed

2 green chillies, finely chopped

10g (¼oz) fresh curry leaves, picked,
  or 1 tablespoon dried curry leaves

3 green cardamom pods, crushed

1 cinnamon stick

2 bay leaves

1 teaspoon sweet smoked paprika

3 tablespoons tomato purée

200g (7oz) tomatoes

1 × 400g (14oz) can coconut milk

200g (7oz) yellow split peas

200g (7oz) red lentils

40g (1½oz) sultanas

salt and pepper

naan or flatbreads (see page 36),
  to serve

FOR THE RADISH PICKLE

1 red onion, sliced

125g (4½oz) radishes, cut into rounds

pinch of caster sugar

1 lemon, halved

salt and pepper

We usually serve this with mango chutney and a crunchy side salad, but you can also keep things simple with just a bowl of rice.

We added this to our menu recently and, rather than include it as a side dish in our Indian range, we put it alongside our other vegetarian mains. Why? Because we think dhal is underappreciated in this country as a main meal. This one is simply bursting with flavours – sweet, savoury, spicy, sour – all in harmony. Don't miss out the easy radish pickle, either – it's well worth it.

Preheat the oven to 200°C fan/220°C/425°F/Gas Mark 7. Place the cauliflower and aubergine in a roasting tray lined with nonstick baking paper. Drizzle with 2 tablespoons of the oil and add half of the garam masala. Season, toss together well and roast for 30 minutes, turning the vegetables halfway through, until they are golden and look delicious. Remove from the oven and place to one side.

Meanwhile, place a medium saucepan or casserole pan on a medium heat. Add the remaining oil followed by the onion, garlic, half of the chillies and half of the curry leaves. Cook for 5–10 minutes, stirring occasionally, until the onions have softened and started to colour. Add the remaining garam masala, along with the cardamom, cinnamon stick, bay leaves and paprika. Stir for 2 minutes to cook out the spices.

Add the tomato purée, tomatoes and coconut milk, then fill the can with water and add that to the pan as well. Add the split peas, lentils and sultanas. Bring to the boil, reduce to a simmer and cook with the lid half-covering the pan for 30–40 minutes, or until the lentils are cooked and the sauce is thickened but there's still quite a bit of liquid. The lentils will catch on the bottom of the pan, so add more water if needed and stir well every so often.

Meanwhile, make the radish pickle. Place the red onion and radishes in a bowl with a good pinch of salt, sugar and juice from ½ lemon. Mix and place to one side.

Once the dhal is ready, fold in most of the roasted vegetables and season to taste. Divide between dishes with the remaining vegetables on top. Cut the remaining lemon half into wedges to serve on the side, along with the radish pickle and naan or flatbreads.

Roasted Mediterranean Vegetable Linguine

PREP: 15 MINUTES · COOK: 30 MINUTES · SERVES 4

2 red onions, cut into thin wedges

2 courgettes, sliced into rounds, then quartered

5 tablespoons olive oil

3 tablespoons balsamic vinegar

finely grated zest and juice of 1 lemon

3 garlic cloves, sliced

300g (10½oz) crème fraîche

200ml (7fl oz) milk

1½ tablespoons cornflour

280g (10oz) dried linguine

1 lemon, cut into wedges

100g (3½oz) feta cheese, crumbled

50g (1¾oz) semi-dried tomatoes in oil, chopped

½ teaspoon dried mixed herbs

salt and pepper

A wonderfully light, flavour-packed pasta dish, especially in summer when courgettes are in season. If you don't have semi-dried tomatoes in your cupboard, add a handful of cherry tomatoes, halved, to the roasting tray with the onions and courgettes. Alternatively, mix a handful of fresh piccolo tomatoes (the sweeter, the better), halved, with the feta.

Preheat the oven to 200°C fan/220°C/425°F/Gas Mark 7.

Place the red onions and courgettes in a roasting tray lined with nonstick baking paper. Drizzle with 2 tablespoons of the oil and add a good pinch of salt and pepper. Roast in the oven for 15 minutes. Add the balsamic vinegar, mix and return to the oven for 10 minutes until the vegetables are roasted and softened.

Meanwhile, place a large frying pan on a low heat. Add 1 tablespoon of the oil, followed by the lemon zest and garlic. Cook for about 2 minutes, stirring, until the garlic is golden. Stir in the crème fraîche and allow to bubble gently and melt. Whisk in the milk and cornflour. Allow to thicken, stirring well, then season to taste and remove from the heat.

Place a large pan of water on to boil and cook the linguine according to the packet instructions. Drain, saving a cup of the pasta water to add to the sauce.

When the vegetables are cooked, tip them into a large bowl and stir the sauce through. Add the cooked linguine and toss with the sauce and vegetables, along with a splash of the reserved pasta water and a squeeze of lemon juice. Season to taste, stir and add more pasta water, if needed.

Mix the feta, semi-dried tomatoes and dried mixed herbs in a bowl with the remaining 1 tablespoon of oil.

Divide the pasta and vegetables between individual dishes and top with the feta and tomato mix. Serve with the remaining lemon wedges for squeezing.

A green salad is all you need on the side. Rocket and watercress with shavings of Parmesan cheese and a balsamic dressing is perfect. For the dressing, simply mix extra virgin olive oil and balsamic vinegar in a ratio of 3:1, with salt and pepper to taste. If you're feeling naughty, you can always add garlic bread on the side.

THE JOY OF GREAT INGREDIENTS

When we started COOK back in 1997, we went to the central London markets for our ingredients – fish from Billingsgate, meat from Smithfield and veg from the greengrocers at New Covent Garden. We figured it was the best way to get great quality, which was all we cared about.

This is no longer how we shop. We've realized we need to care about a lot more than just quality. We've grown increasingly aware of how many of the world's biggest challenges appear on our plates. Nature, climate, poverty, energy, community, health, equality – these are all food issues.

To make progress on any of them, we need to get closer to where our food comes from. Wendell Berry – an American farmer, poet, environmental activist and all-round dude – summed it up when he said, 'Eating is an agricultural act.' As lovers of good food, we need to seek to understand and support our farmers better. We might even need to pay them more for the ingredients we cook with.

Providing cheap, plentiful food has been the driving force behind farming since the end of the Second World War. As others have pointed out, where we've ended up is both a miracle and a disaster – a miracle because food is, by any historical measure, both absurdly cheap and plentiful, but a disaster because we've ignored the consequences for our health, for nature and for farmers. Changing direction is going to be hard because there are no easy answers. But change we must.

It's easy to become gloomy about the outlook. But, once again, we can look to Wendell Berry for guidance. 'Be joyful though you have considered all the facts,' he advises in his poem 'The Mad Farmer Liberation Front'. Absolutely.

There are so many inspiring, passionate farmers doing remarkable things to make a difference in their small corner of the land. We're fortunate to work with some of them at COOK and are always looking for more. Because when you know and trust how an ingredient has been grown, cared for and harvested, it tastes just a little bit better. And your meal comes with an extra sprinkling of joy.

DIG IN – Recommended Reading

'The Pleasures of Eating', an essay by Wendell Berry from *What Are People For?*, Farrar Straus & Giroux, 1990

Dirt to Soil: One family's journey into regenerative agriculture, Gabe Brown, Chelsea Green Publishing, Vermont, 2018

Ravenous: How to get ourselves and our planet into shape, Henry Dimbleby, Profile Books, London 2023

English Pastoral: An inheritance, James Rebanks, Allen Lane, London, 2020

The Way We Eat Now: Strategies for eating in a world of change, Bee Wilson, Fourth Estate, London, 2019

ffcc.co.uk – Great free resources online from the UK's Food, Farming and Countryside Commission

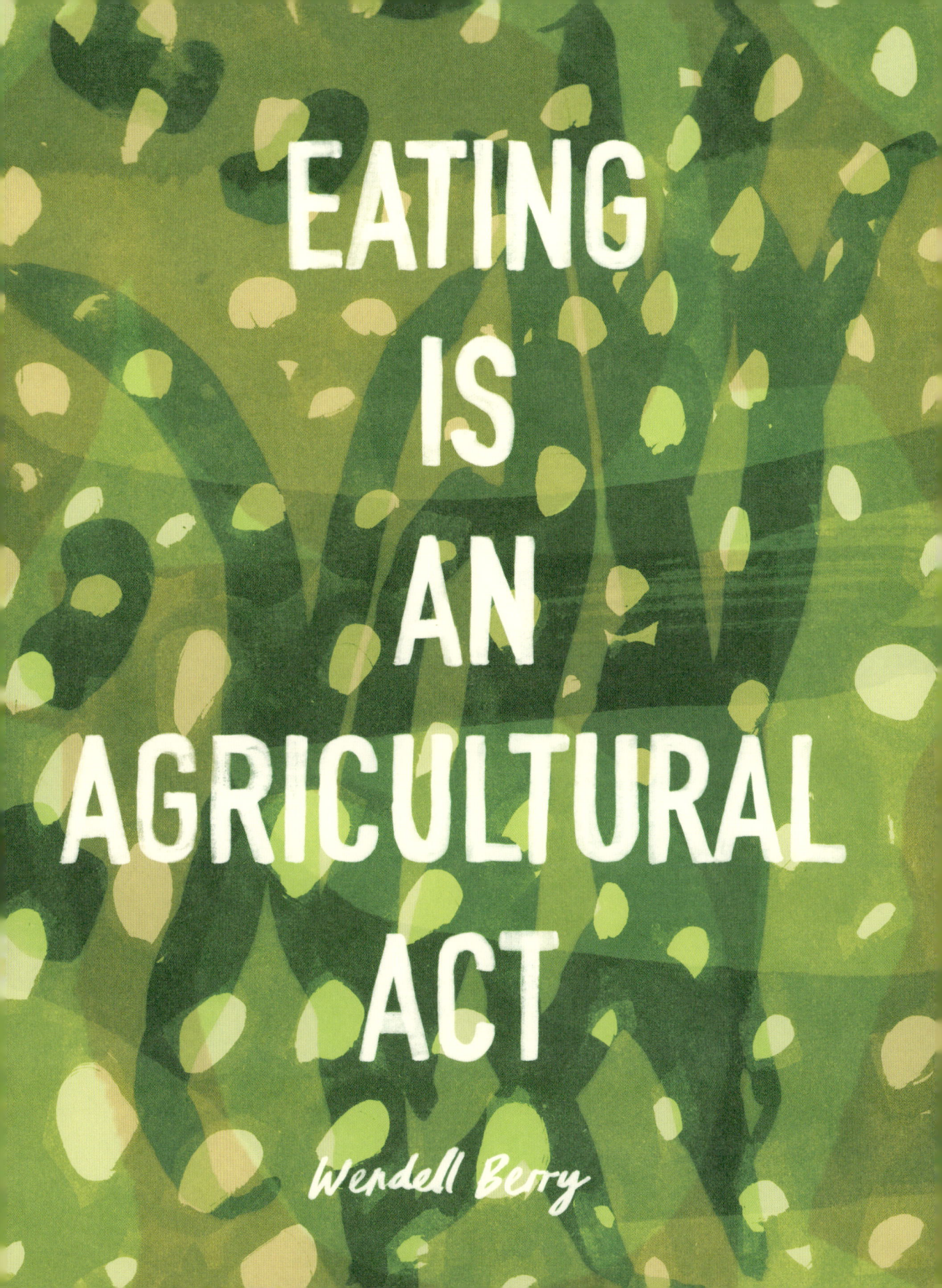

'It is more important
to be together than
in agreement'

– Pedro Tarek

KITCHEN WISDOM NO.2

Feeding the Family

No, it's not just you. Family mealtimes can be excruciating ... and sometimes wonderful.

Here are our best recipes (and learnings) for keeping everybody happy.

Chicken, Ham and Leek Pie

PREP: 35 MINUTES · COOK: 1 HOUR 25 MINUTES, PLUS 20 MINUTES COOLING TIME · SERVES 4–6

FOR THE PASTRY

250g (9oz) plain flour, plus extra
    for dusting
pinch of salt
125g (4½oz) cold, unsalted butter, cut
    into cubes, plus extra for greasing
1½ tablespoons cold water
2 egg yolks

FOR THE FILLING

2 tablespoons rapeseed oil
40g (1½oz) unsalted butter
2 onions, finely sliced
2 leeks, trimmed, cleaned and
    finely sliced
2 tablespoons picked thyme
5 skinless, boneless chicken thighs,
    about 500g (1lb 2oz), sliced
2 tablespoon plain flour
100ml (3½fl oz) white wine
300ml (10fl oz) chicken stock
100ml (3½fl oz) double cream
250g (9 oz) cooked gammon
    ham, diced
2 tablespoons chopped flat leaf parsley
salt and pepper

*Make full use of the oven and roast
some new potatoes on the shelf below
your pie as well as some broccoli
florets. Trim the florets to a uniform
size and spread them out on a baking
tray, drizzle with olive oil and season,
then roast for about 20 minutes.
Remove from the oven and grate over
some lemon zest and Parmesan…
you'll be hooked.*

It is a truth universally acknowledged that nobody is ever disappointed when you say 'It's Chicken, Ham and Leek Pie for supper.' This has been one of our bestsellers since the very beginning. And, yes, using shop-bought pastry is definitely allowed if you don't want to make your own (life's too short). If you can't find cooked gammon ham, use smoked bacon lardons and fry them with the onions and leeks.

To make the pastry, place the flour in a food processor with a pinch of salt. Add the butter and pulse to combine until it reaches a chunky breadcrumb texture. Add the measured water and 1 egg yolk, then pulse again to form a soft dough. Turn out on a clean surface and pat into a disc shape. Wrap in clingfilm and place in the fridge to rest.

Meanwhile, make the pie filling. Place a large, shallow casserole pan on a medium heat. Add the oil and butter, followed by the onions, leeks and most of the thyme (reserving a little for sprinkling over the finished pie). Cook for 10 minutes, stirring occasionally, or until the onions are translucent. Increase the heat and add the chicken. Cook for 5 minutes, or until the chicken is turning golden.

Now add the flour, give everything in the pan a good stir and cook for 1–2 minutes. Add the wine, allow to reduce for 2 minutes, then add the chicken stock and stir well. Bring to the boil, then reduce to a simmer for about 15 minutes. Stir in the cream, ham and parsley, then simmer for a further 5–10 minutes if the sauce needs to thicken. Turn the heat off and leave to cool.

Preheat the oven to 200°C fan/220°C/425°F/Gas Mark 7. Place a baking sheet in the oven to heat up.

You will need a 25cm (10 inch) circular pie dish. Take the pastry from the fridge, unwrap it and place it on a lightly floured surface. Roll out the pastry to a circle 6mm (¼ inch) thick – it should be larger than your pie dish. Transfer the chicken filling to the pie dish. Lightly beat the remaining egg yolk in a small bowl and brush some of this around the edge of the pie dish, then drape the pastry over the top. Trim the pastry so it's a little larger than the circumference of the dish and crimp it around the outside. You can use any remaining pastry to make decorations for the top of the pie. Cut a little slit in the centre. Brush the pie with the remaining beaten egg yolk and sprinkle over the reserved thyme.

Place the dish on the hot baking sheet and bake in the oven for 40–45 minutes, or until golden. Allow the pie to sit for 5 minutes before slicing and serving.

Meatballs in a Rustic Tomato Sauce

PREP: 20 MINUTES · COOK: 1 HOUR 30 MINUTES · SERVES 6 (MAKES 16–20 MEATBALLS)

FOR THE MEATBALLS
85g (3oz) fresh breadcrumbs

2 tablespoons milk

1 egg

300g (10½oz) minced beef

300g (10½oz) minced pork

½ onion, finely chopped

2 garlic cloves, crushed

2 tablespoons red pesto

15g (½oz) basil, leaves picked
    and chopped

¼ teaspoon ground white pepper

½ teaspoon dried chilli flakes

½ teaspoon salt

2 tablespoons olive oil

Parmesan cheese, to serve

FOR THE SAUCE
2 tablespoons olive oil

20g (¾oz) unsalted butter

1 onion, finely chopped

1 carrot, finely chopped

1 celery stick, finely chopped

2 garlic cloves, crushed

200ml (7fl oz) red wine

50g (1¾oz) semi-dried tomatoes
    in oil, chopped

3 tablespoons tomato purée

400ml (14fl oz) chicken stock

1 tablespoon malt vinegar

2 tablespoons balsamic vinegar

1 tablespoon light soft brown sugar

2 × 400g (14oz) cans chopped
    tomatoes

15g (½oz) basil, leaves picked
    and chopped

salt and pepper

Here, the humble meatball is elevated to a thing of beauty – or, at least, a high-class supper. Years ago, we discovered an ice-cream scoop was the perfect size for making meatballs – give it a go. If you're cooking from frozen, cover with tin foil and cook for 1 hour at 170°C fan/190°C/375°F/ Gas Mark 5, then remove the foil and cook for a further 15 minutes to allow the meatballs to colour.

Start by making the meatballs. Line a tray or plate with nonstick baking paper. Place the breadcrumbs in a large bowl and add the milk and egg. Mix, then set to one side for a few minutes to soak. Add the minced beef and pork, onion, garlic, pesto, basil, white pepper, chilli flakes and salt. Scrunch everything together with your hands to combine. Using damp hands, divide the mixture into 16–20 balls (each weighing about 40g/1½oz). Place on the tray, cover and place in the fridge until needed.

To make the sauce, place a large, shallow, ovenproof casserole pan on a medium heat. Add the oil and butter. When the butter has melted, add the onion, carrot, celery and garlic. Cook, stirring continuously, for 10 minutes, or until the onions are cooked but not coloured. Increase the heat, add the red wine and allow to bubble and reduce by half.

Reduce the heat and stir in the semi-dried tomatoes, tomato purée, chicken stock, vinegars, sugar and chopped tomatoes. Increase the heat again and bring to the boil, then reduce to a simmer and allow to cook for 30 minutes, or until thickened.

When you're ready to cook the meatballs, preheat the oven to 180°C fan/200°C/ 400°F/Gas Mark 6. Take the meatballs from the fridge and place a large frying pan on a medium heat. Coat the meatballs in the oil, then add them to the pan to brown all over. You will need to do this in batches.

When the sauce has finished cooking, season to taste and stir through the basil. Add the browned meatballs to the pan. Place the pan in the oven, uncovered, and allow to cook for 20–30 minutes, or until the sauce is bubbling and the meatballs are golden and cooked through.

Bring the pan to the table, grate over a generous helping of Parmesan and serve.

Serve with either linguine or spaghetti, with some crusty bread for mopping up the sauce and a green salad on the side (ideally with a few basil leaves thrown in).

Sticky Barbecue Ribs

PREP: 10 MINUTES · COOK: 2 HOURS 15 MINUTES–3 HOURS 15 MINUTES · SERVES 4

FOR THE RIBS

2 × racks pork baby back ribs, about
    500g (1lb 2oz) each
4 garlic cloves, crushed
100g (3½oz) soft dark brown sugar
1 teaspoon salt

FOR THE SAUCE

3 garlic cloves, crushed
3 tablespoon clear honey
3 tablespoons tomato purée
2 tablespoon English mustard
1 teaspoon sweet smoked paprika
½ teaspoon chilli flakes
100ml (3½fl oz) white wine vinegar
50ml (2fl oz) dark soy sauce
50ml (2fl oz) light soy sauce
2 tablespoons soft dark brown sugar
200ml (7fl oz) apple juice
pepper

A truly epic recipe that we sadly no longer make. The secret is to braise the ribs slowly, then baste with the beautiful, sticky barbecue sauce, before roasting at a high heat to finish. We used paint brushes to do the basting in the kitchen, hundreds of racks at a time! You can use (cheap) beer instead of water for the slow cook, which adds a lovely hoppy flavour.

Preheat the oven to 140°C fan/160°C/325°F/Gas Mark 3. Place the ribs in a snug-fitting roasting tray. Pour over enough water to just cover the ribs, then add the garlic, sugar and salt. Cover well with a double layer of tin foil and roast in the oven for 2–3 hours, turning the ribs halfway through, until the meat is tender but not falling apart.

Meanwhile, make the barbecue sauce. Place all the ingredients in a medium-sized saucepan, bring to the boil, then reduce to a simmer on a low heat, stirring frequently. After about 20 minutes, once the sauce coats the back of a spoon, turn off the heat.

When the ribs are cooked, remove from the oven and carefully drain away the cooking water. Increase the oven temperature to 200°C fan/220°C/425°F/Gas Mark 7. Baste the ribs all over with the sauce and return to the oven. Cook for about 15 minutes, turning and basting the ribs in the sauce every few minutes, or until the ribs are sticky and the sauce is starting to crisp a little on the surface. Remove from the oven, slice into individual ribs and serve.

If you wish, you can finish the ribs on a barbecue, rather than in the oven, for the last 15 minutes. Just baste and turn regularly until they're sticky and delicious. To serve, sprinkle over some sliced chilli and spring onions, and crushed peanuts.

Piri-piri Drumsticks Traybake

PREP: 20 MINUTES, PLUS MARINATING · COOK: 1 HOUR · SERVES 4

FOR THE MARINATED CHICKEN

8 chicken drumsticks, about 800g
(1lb 12oz) total weight

3 red peppers, cored, deseeded
and sliced

2 red onions, cut into wedges

2 teaspoons dried oregano

2 teaspoons sweet smoked paprika

2 tablespoons rapeseed oil

salt and pepper

4 tablespoons chopped flat leaf
parsley, to garnish

FOR THE SAUCE

1 fresh red chilli, halved and deseeded

1 red onion, finely chopped

3 vine-ripened tomatoes,
roughly chopped

2 garlic cloves, finely chopped

3 tablespoons tomato purée

50ml (2fl oz) white wine vinegar

3 tablespoons light soft brown sugar

salt and pepper

It's hard not to appreciate the splendour of a piri-piri-style sauce – tangy, sweet and spicy, all at once. This is a recipe from our archives, with the sauce made from scratch. It means you can experiment with the spice and flavour levels to find your perfect pitch.

———————————————————————

Prick the chicken all over with a metal skewer. Place the drumsticks in an extra-large freezer bag with the peppers, onions, dried herbs and oil. Season with a good pinch each of salt and pepper. Massage the contents of the bag to ensure the chicken is well covered in the marinade, then seal the bag and place in the fridge. Allow the flavours to mingle for at least 4 hours, but preferably overnight.

When you're ready to cook, preheat the oven to 180°C fan/200°C/400°F/ Gas Mark 6. Tip the chicken, peppers and onions into a large roasting tray. Bake in the oven for 30 minutes.

Meanwhile, make the sauce. Place the chilli and onion in a blender and blitz until smooth. Add all the remaining sauce ingredients and blitz again until smooth.

Remove the tray of chicken from the oven and pour the sauce around the chicken and vegetables. Return the tray to the oven and cook for a further 30 minutes, or until the chicken is tender and cooked through. When ready, remove from the oven, sprinkle over the chopped parsley and serve.

Sweet potato wedges are the perfect accompaniment. Just slice 3 sweet potatoes into wedges (no need to peel, but do give them a good scrub first), toss in some olive oil, season with a pinch of paprika and salt, and roast in the oven (same temperature as the chicken) for about 40 minutes. Otherwise, flatbreads (see page 36) or rice and a dressed salad does the trick.

Lasagne al Forno

PREP: 30 MINUTES · COOK: 3 HOURS · SERVES 4

150g (5½oz) fresh egg lasagne
    sheets (about 9 sheets)

FOR THE RAGU

2 tablespoons olive oil, plus extra
    for greasing
1 carrot, finely chopped
1 onion, finely chopped
1 celery stick, finely chopped
2 garlic cloves, crushed
1 tablespoon dried oregano
30g (1oz) basil, leaves picked and
    stalks chopped
200g (7oz) minced pork (at least
    10% fat for flavour)
200g (7oz) minced beef (at least
    10% fat for flavour)
3 tablespoons red wine vinegar
4 tablespoons tomato purée
1 tablespoon light soft brown sugar
2 × 400g (14oz) cans chopped
    tomatoes
salt and pepper

FOR THE CHEESE SAUCE

600ml (20fl oz) milk
a little grated nutmeg
50g (1¾oz) unsalted butter
50g (1¾oz) plain flour
2 teaspoons English mustard
200g (7oz) mature Cheddar
    cheese, grated
salt and pepper

The don of family dinner times. Using beef and pork mince brings a distinctive flavour and makes it less like just a layered Bolognese sauce. When it comes to the cheese topping, go big or go home. There's nothing remotely Italian about Cheddar but, when it tastes so good, who cares? Having ragu in the freezer is like a gift from the gods – it can be used in so many different ways – so definitely make extra to freeze, if you can.

Place a large casserole dish on a medium heat. Add the oil, followed by the carrot, onion, celery, garlic, oregano and basil stalks. Cook for about 10 minutes, stirring continuously, until the onion has become translucent. Increase the heat a little and add the pork and beef. Brown the meat, breaking up any big lumps with a wooden spoon, for 10 minutes, or until the meat is golden brown all over.

Add the vinegar and allow to bubble for 1 minute. Add 3 tablespoons of the tomato purée, the sugar and the chopped tomatoes, then half-fill one of the cans with water and add that to the pan as well. Bring to the boil, then reduce the heat to low, leave the lid slightly ajar and simmer for about 2 hours, stirring occasionally, until the sauce has reduced and thickened slightly. Season to taste.

Meanwhile, make the cheese sauce. Gently warm the milk with a few gratings of nutmeg in a small saucepan on a low heat. Place a medium saucepan on a medium–low heat and add the butter. Allow it to melt, then stir in the flour. Cook, still stirring, for 2 minutes, or until the paste starts to bubble. Using a ladle, gradually add the warm milk. Keep stirring to form a smooth sauce. Stir in the mustard and most of the cheese, reserving a little for the topping. Season to taste.

Chop the basil leaves and mix in a small bowl with the reserved cheese and the remaining tablespoon of tomato purée to make the topping.

Preheat the oven to 180°C fan/200°C/400°F/Gas Mark 6. Grease a 28 × 20cm (11 × 8 inch) deep, ovenproof dish with olive oil. Spoon one-third of the ragu into the dish and top with 3 lasagne sheets. Add one-third of the cheese sauce and another third of the ragu, followed by 3 more lasagne sheets. Repeat with another third of the cheese sauce, the remainder of the ragu and a final layer of lasagne sheets. Top with the remaining cheese sauce, then sprinkle over the topping.

Bake in the oven for 30 minutes, or until bubbling and golden. Allow the lasagne to settle for 10 minutes before diving in.

Mushroom and Aubergine Lasagne

PREP: 40 MINUTES · COOK: 1 HOUR 45 MINUTES · SERVES 4–6

1 tablespoon rapeseed oil,
    plus extra for greasing

1 teaspoon fennel seeds, crushed

2 medium aubergines, chopped

200g (7oz) chestnut mushrooms,
    trimmed and quartered

1 tablespoon light soy sauce

½ teaspoon ground white pepper

150g (5½oz) dried lasagne sheets

a little olive oil

5g (⅛oz) fresh breadcrumbs

1 rosemary sprig, leaves picked
    and chopped

10g (¼oz) pine nuts

10g (¼oz) semi-dried tomatoes in oil,
    chopped (optional)

salt and pepper

FOR THE TOMATO SAUCE

1 tablespoon rapeseed oil

1 onion, finely chopped

2 celery sticks, finely chopped

1 carrot, finely chopped

10g (¼oz) fresh mixed herbs, chopped

3 garlic cloves, chopped

2 tablespoons tomato purée

2 × 400g (14oz) cans chopped tomatoes

850ml (1½ pints) vegetable stock

100g (3½oz) dried green or brown
    lentils, rinsed

50g (1¾oz) cashew nuts, chopped

FOR THE WHITE SAUCE

300ml (10fl oz) plant-based milk

30g (1oz) vegan butter

30g (1oz) plain flour

1 teaspoon English mustard

a little grated nutmeg

A plant-based lasagne that will knock your socks off, with a lovely depth of flavour and a big umami hit.

Grease a 25 × 30cm (10 × 12 inch) ovenproof dish with a little rapeseed oil. Preheat the oven to 180°C fan/200°C/400°F/Gas Mark 6.

First, make the tomato sauce. Place a large saucepan on a medium heat. Add the oil, onion, celery, carrot, herbs and garlic. Cook, stirring occasionally, for about 10 minutes until softened. Stir in the tomato purée, canned tomatoes, stock, lentils and cashew nuts. Bring to the boil, then reduce the heat to the lowest setting and cook for 1 hour until the sauce is thickened and the lentils are cooked. Stir the contents of the pan regularly to stop the lentils from sticking. Season to taste.

Meanwhile, place the fennel seeds, aubergines, mushrooms, soy sauce and white pepper in a roasting tray, toss together with the tablespoon of rapeseed oil and roast in the oven for 40 minutes until softened and golden. Remove from the oven and place to one side.

Now make the white sauce. Gently warm the plant-based milk in a small saucepan on a low heat. Place a medium saucepan on a low heat, then add the vegan butter. When it's melted, stir in the flour. Cook, still stirring, for 2 minutes, or until the paste starts to bubble. Using a ladle, gradually add the warm milk, whisking between each addition to form a smooth sauce. Stir in the mustard and a few gratings of nutmeg. Season to taste.

Meanwhile, pre-cook the lasagne sheets in salted boiling water for 8 minutes. Drain, run under cold water, then drizzle with olive oil to prevent sticking.

Mix together the breadcrumbs, rosemary, pine nuts and semi-dried tomatoes (if using) in a bowl to make the topping.

To assemble the lasagne, spoon one-third of the tomato sauce into the prepared dish and top with one-third of the vegetables and 3 lasagne sheets. Repeat with another third of the sauce and the vegetables and 3 more lasagne sheets, then repeat with a final layer. Top with the white sauce and sprinkle over the topping. Bake in the oven for 30 minutes, or until golden and bubbling. Allow to stand for 10 minutes before serving.

Serve with a classic rocket salad dressed with a squeeze of lemon juice, a drizzle of olive oil and shavings of vegan Parmesan.

Vegetable Lasagne

PREP: 45 MINUTES · COOK: 1 HOUR 45 MINUTES · SERVES 6

FOR THE VEGETABLES

1 tablespoon rapeseed oil,
    plus extra for greasing
200g (7oz) chestnut mushrooms,
    trimmed and sliced
2 courgettes, sliced into half moons
6 thyme sprigs, leaves picked
200g (7oz) baby spinach

FOR THE TOMATO AND
RED PEPPER SAUCE

2 tablespoons rapeseed oil
2 red onions, finely chopped
5 garlic cloves, crushed
1 carrot, finely chopped
1 celery stick, finely chopped
1 tablespoon dried sage
20g (¾oz) flat leaf parsley, chopped
2 tablespoons dried basil
2 tablespoons tomato purée
250g (9oz) roasted red peppers
    in oil, diced
1 × 400g (14oz) can chopped tomatoes

FOR THE CHEESE SAUCE

300ml (10fl oz) milk
30g (1oz) butter
30g (1oz) plain flour
100g (3½oz) mascarpone cheese
100g (3½oz) ricotta cheese or
    crème fraîche

FOR THE LASAGNE

100g (3½ oz) mature Cheddar
    cheese, grated
125g (4½oz) fresh egg lasagne sheets
    (7–8 sheets)
salt and pepper

There are many committed carnivores for whom our Roasted Vegetable Lasagne is their hands-down favourite dish. Rather than roasting the veg, as we do in our kitchen, here we're cooking on the hob to save time (the flavour's just as good).

Place a large nonstick frying pan on a medium heat. Add the oil, followed by the mushrooms, courgettes and thyme. Fry for 10 minutes until the vegetables are turning golden. Stir in the spinach and allow to wilt. Season well, then turn off the heat and leave to cool. Chop the vegetables into smaller pieces, then place in a bowl to one side.

Meanwhile, make the tomato and red pepper sauce. Place a large nonstick saucepan on a medium heat. Add the oil along with the onions, garlic, carrot, celery, sage, most of the parsley (reserving a little for later on) and half of the basil. Cook for 10 minutes, or until the onions are translucent. Add the tomato purée, most of the red peppers (reserving some for the topping) and the chopped tomatoes, then half-fill the can with water and add that to the pan as well. Bring to the boil, then reduce to a simmer for 30–40 minutes.

Meanwhile, make the cheese sauce. Gently warm the milk in a small saucepan on a low heat. Place a medium saucepan on a low heat, then add the butter. When it's melted, stir in the flour. Cook, still stirring, for 2 minutes, or until the paste starts to bubble. Using a ladle, gradually add the warm milk, whisking between each addition, to form a smooth, thick sauce. Stir in the mascarpone and the ricotta or crème fraîche. Season to taste.

Mix together the grated Cheddar, reserved peppers and remaining basil in a bowl to make the topping. Season with pepper. Preheat the oven to 180°C fan/200°C/400°F/Gas Mark 6. Grease a 20 × 30cm (8 × 12 inch) ovenproof dish with a little rapeseed oil.

Season the tomato sauce to taste, sprinkle in most of the remaining parsley, then spoon half the sauce into the prepared dish. Top with a layer of lasagne sheets. Scatter the vegetables over the pasta. Top with the remaining tomato sauce and a second layer of pasta, then spoon over the cheese sauce. Sprinkle over the topping. Bake in the oven for 35–40 minutes, or until golden and bubbling. Allow to stand for 5 minutes before serving, sprinkled with the remaining parsley.

Chilli Con Carne

PREP: 15 MINUTES · COOK: 1 HOUR 50 MINUTES–2 HOURS 20 MINUTES · SERVES 4

1 tablespoon dried oregano

1 tablespoon dried basil

2 tablespoons ground cumin

1 tablespoon ground coriander

1 tablespoon sweet smoked paprika

1 tablespoon garlic powder or garlic salt

1 teaspoon ground cinnamon

1 teaspoon dried chilli flakes

2 tablespoons rapeseed oil

1 onion, finely chopped

2 garlic cloves, finely chopped

30g (1oz) fresh coriander, leaves
picked and stalks chopped

250g (9oz) minced beef

20g (¾oz) unsalted butter

3 tablespoons tomato purée

300ml (10fl oz) beef stock

2 × 400g (14oz) cans chopped
tomatoes

1 × 400g (14oz) can cannellini
beans, drained

1 × 400g (14oz) can kidney beans,
drained

1 tablespoon cocoa powder

salt and pepper

TO GARNISH (OPTIONAL)

1 fresh chilli, finely sliced

sliced avocado

thinly sliced red onion

A big, bold, complex chilli recipe that's won loads of awards. The cocoa powder adds a wonderful richness and, if you're feeling flush, you can take it up a level by using a couple of pieces of good-quality dark chocolate instead. Chilli and chocolate are a match made in heaven.

Put all the dried herbs and spices in a small bowl, mix and place to one side.

Place a large saucepan or casserole dish on a medium heat. Add the oil, onion, garlic and coriander stalks. Cook for 5 minutes, stirring, until the onions are translucent. Increase the heat and add the beef. Brown the beef for about 10 minutes, using a wooden spoon to break up the bigger pieces. Reduce the heat to medium and add the butter, followed by all the dried herbs and spices. Stir and cook for about 1 minute, then add the tomato purée, stock, chopped tomatoes, beans and cocoa powder. Give it a good stir.

Bring to the boil, then reduce to a simmer. Put the lid on the pan, but slightly ajar, and cook for 1½–2 hours, stirring from time to time, or until thickened and smelling delicious. Season to taste. Divide between bowls and sprinkle with the chopped coriander leaves and chilli, avocado and red onion slices (if using).

CHILLI CON VEGGIE

To make a deliciously meat-free version, swap in 300g (10½oz) Quorn mince and vegetable stock. Follow the recipe above, adding 1 × 160g (5¾oz) can sweetcorn (drained) along with the chopped tomatoes. Serve the chilli con veggie with lime wedges, as well as the coriander leaves and chilli slices (if using).

You can keep it simple with rice, tortillas or a jacket potato, but we love to make a bigger spread with guacamole, salsa, sour cream, grated cheese and a crunchy salad. According to Hannah in our design team, a foolproof guacamole ratio is for every 1 avocado, add 6 cherry tomatoes, finely chopped, ¼ red onion, finely chopped, and a handful of fresh coriander. Mash it all together with the juice of ½ lime and a pinch of sea salt.

Toad in the Hole with Red Onion Chutney

PREP: 10 MINUTES · COOK: 1 HOUR 15 MINUTES · SERVES 4

3 tablespoons rapeseed oil

3 red onions, finely sliced

2 garlic cloves, finely chopped

2 tablespoons picked thyme

100ml (3½fl oz) balsamic vinegar

2 tablespoons light soft brown sugar

8 Lincolnshire pork sausages

1 tablespoon chopped rosemary

2 eggs

125g (4½oz) plain flour

125ml (4fl oz) milk

salt and pepper

Is there a better-named British dish? Sausages in crisp and fluffy Yorkshire pudding, with the origins going back to the 18th century. To this day, our co-founder Dale laments that he could never crack freezing Yorkshire pudding batter properly ... which is why we only had this on our menu for a couple of years.

Preheat the oven to 210°C fan/230°C/450°F/Gas Mark 8.

Place a medium saucepan on a medium heat. Add 2 tablespoons of the oil along with the onions, garlic and thyme. Reduce the heat to low and cook for 15–20 minutes, stirring occasionally, until the onions are softened. Add the vinegar and sugar, then increase the heat to medium. Allow to bubble for 2 minutes, then reduce the heat to low again. Let the vinegar reduce until it has nearly evaporated and the sugar has melted. Turn off the heat, then pour the red onion chutney into a bowl and place to one side.

Meanwhile, take a 20 × 26cm (8 × 10½ inch) roasting tray and pour in the remaining tablespoon of oil. Place in the hot oven for 5 minutes to heat up, then carefully add the sausages and rosemary and return the tray to the oven. Cook the sausages for 15–20 minutes, or until just cooked.

Meanwhile, place the eggs, flour, milk and a pinch of salt in a large measuring jug. Whisk well to a smooth batter.

When the sausages are ready, remove the tray from the oven. Carefully and quickly pour the batter around the sausages. Return the tray to the oven for 25 minutes, or until the batter is golden and slightly risen. Don't be tempted to open the oven door while it's cooking!

Serve immediately with the red onion chutney on the side.

Smoked Haddock Gratin

PREP: 35 MINUTES · COOK: 1 HOUR 15 MINUTES · SERVES 4

300g (10½oz) potatoes, peeled and
    cut into bite-sized pieces

300g (10½oz) sweet potatoes, peeled
    and cut into bite-sized pieces

2 tablespoons rapeseed oil

1 tablespoon picked thyme

500ml (18fl oz) milk

2 bay leaves

400g (14oz) undyed smoked
    haddock fillets

115g (4oz) bacon lardons

1 small onion, chopped

½ red chilli, finely chopped

50g (1¾oz) butter

50g (1¾oz) plain flour

30ml (1fl oz) double cream

finely grated zest of 1 lemon

1 × 198g (7oz) can sweetcorn, drained

150g (5½oz) broccoli, cut into
    small florets

50g (1¾oz) mature Cheddar
    cheese, grated

¼ teaspoon paprika

salt and pepper

*Serve with buttered garden peas
and lots of crusty bread to mop up
the sauce. Add some spicy sauce –
like sriracha or Tabasco – to the
table, for folks who like things hot.*

A COOK original that started out life as a jambalaya before morphing into a golden-topped gratin. It's got a bit of everything going on – saltiness, creaminess, pops of sweetness, vibrant veg, a little heat and a comforting potato and cheese topping.

Preheat the oven to 180°C fan/200°C/400°F/Gas Mark 6.

In a bowl, toss the potatoes and the sweet potatoes with the oil and thyme. Season, then spread out on a baking tray and roast in the top of the oven for about 15 minutes until lightly coloured and still retaining a slight bite. Remove from the oven and place to one side. Reduce the oven temperature to 170°C fan/190°C/375°F/Gas Mark 5.

Add the milk and bay leaves to a large nonstick frying pan. Add the fish, skin-side down, cover and bring to a gentle simmer over a medium heat. Cook for 4–5 minutes until the fish is opaque and starting to flake into pieces. Turn the heat off and leave the fish to stand in the milk for 5 minutes. Lift the fish onto a plate, flake into large pieces and place in a 20 × 25cm (8 × 10 inch) baking dish. Strain the poaching milk into a jug and place to one side.

Wipe the frying pan clean and add the bacon lardons. Put the pan on a medium–high heat. Cook for 10–15 minutes until brown and crisp, then carefully remove the bacon from the pan using a slotted spoon so that the fat stays in the pan. Place the bacon onto kitchen paper to absorb any excess fat and oil, then scatter on top of the flaked haddock. Add the onion and chilli to the pan with the rendered bacon fat. Cook on a medium heat for 3–4 minutes until the onions are soft and translucent. Transfer to a plate and place to one side.

Wipe the frying pan clean again and add the butter. When it's melted, stir in the flour and cook for 1 minute over a medium heat. Take off the heat, pour in a little of the poaching milk, then stir until smooth. Continue to add the milk gradually, mixing well, until you have a smooth sauce. Stir in the cream and lemon zest, followed by the onions and chilli. Cook over a low heat for 2 minutes, stirring continuously. Season to taste and remove from the heat.

Add the sweetcorn and broccoli to the haddock and bacon, cover with the sauce, then spread the potatoes in an even layer on top. Sprinkle over the Cheddar and paprika. Bake in the oven for 20 minutes, until golden and bubbling around the edges.

Classic Fish Pie

PREP: 30 MINUTES · COOK: 1 HOUR 15 MINUTES · SERVES 4–6

FOR THE MASHED POTATO

50g (1¾oz) unsalted butter,
    plus extra for greasing

1.5kg (3lb 5oz) potatoes suitable
    for mashing, peeled and chopped
    into equal-sized pieces

½ teaspoon ground white pepper

2 egg yolks

1 teaspoon dried paprika

salt

FOR THE FILLING

250ml (9fl oz) fish stock

50g (1¾oz) unsalted butter

1 onion, finely chopped

2 bay leaves

50g (1¾oz) plain flour

100ml (3½fl oz) dry white wine

50ml (2fl oz) dry sherry or Pernod

250ml (9fl oz) milk

200ml (7fl oz) double cream

3 tablespoons finely chopped flat leaf
    parsley, plus extra for serving

2 tablespoons lemon juice

175g (6oz) raw king prawns

300g (10½oz) salmon fillet, skinned,
    deboned and chopped into chunks

300g (10½oz) haddock, skinned,
    deboned and chopped into chunks

salt and pepper

½ lemon, cut into wedges, to serve

Serve with something vibrant and green – spring greens, buttered garden peas or roasted broccoli.

A true COOK classic. Over the years, we've toyed with changing the trademark, diagonal stripes of paprika on top – they're a bit retro, after all. But no matter what trendier or tastier options we come up with, we always return to the stripes. We've now arrived at acceptance. As the sage Dolly Parton once said: 'Find out who you are and do it on purpose.' If you're planning to freeze this dish, leave your mash and sauce to cool completely before folding in the fish, to ensure it doesn't overcook.

Grease a 30 × 20cm (12 × 8 inch) ovenproof dish with butter.

Place the potatoes in a large saucepan of salted water. Bring to the boil and simmer for about 15 minutes, or until the potatoes are cooked through. Drain in a colander over the sink and allow the potatoes to steam dry a little.

Place the pan back on the hob on a low heat and add the butter. When it's melted, return the potatoes to the pan and add the white pepper and a good pinch of salt. Mash the potatoes well until smooth. Remove from the heat, add the egg yolks and mash again. Cover the pan and place to one side.

Now make the filling. Heat the fish stock in a small saucepan on a low heat. Place a large saucepan on a low heat and add the butter. When it's melted, add the onion and bay leaves. Cook on low, stirring continuously, for about 5 minutes, or until the onion is translucent. Add the flour and cook, still stirring, for 2 minutes, or until the paste starts to bubble. Pour in the white wine and sherry or Pernod, allow to bubble, then stir in the hot stock. Keep stirring until smooth; a whisk will really help. Gradually whisk in the milk to form a smooth sauce. Stir in the double cream, parsley and lemon juice. Season to taste and remove from the heat, discarding the bay leaves.

Preheat the oven to 180°C fan/200°C/400°F/Gas Mark 6.

Fold the prawns and fish into the sauce. Spoon the sauce into the prepared dish. Pipe or spoon the mashed potato on top. You can use a fork to create lines in the mash. Sprinkle little lines of paprika in between the piped potato or fork lines. Place the dish on a baking tray and bake in the oven for 30 minutes, or until golden and bubbling. Allow to sit for 5 minutes before serving.

Scatter over a little more parsley and serve with lemon wedges on the side.

Smoked Haddock and Welsh Rarebit Fishcakes

PREP: 10 MINUTES, PLUS RESTING TIME IN FRIDGE · COOK: 1 HOUR · SERVES 4 (MAKES 8 FISHCAKES)

700ml (1¼ pint) milk

3 bay leaves

6 black peppercorns

500g (1lb 2oz) undyed smoked
    haddock fillets

750g (1lb 10oz) Maris Piper potatoes,
    chopped (skin left on)

20g (¾oz) unsalted butter

4 tablespoons chopped flat leaf parsley

2 lemons

1 teaspoon English mustard

2 teaspoons wholegrain mustard

50g (1¾oz) mature Cheddar
    cheese, grated

1 tablespoon Worcestershire sauce

¼ teaspoon ground white pepper

100g (3½oz) plain flour

3 eggs, beaten

200g (7oz) fresh breadcrumbs

2 tablespoons olive oil

salt and pepper

The classic Welsh Rarebit ingredients running through the mash here create a perfect backdrop for generous flakes of salty, smoky haddock. It's a great recipe that we only had on our menu for a couple of years. You can, of course, swap in whatever fish you like: fresh haddock, cod, salmon... Or use ready-to-eat fish fillets to save time.

___

Place the milk, bay leaves and peppercorns in a medium frying pan. Place on a low heat and allow the milk to steam gently but not bubble and burn. Once the milk is steaming, add the haddock and poach for 8–10 minutes until soft. Transfer the haddock to a shallow bowl using a fish slice and place to one side. Keep 100ml (3½fl oz) of the poaching milk for the mashed potato.

Place the potatoes in a large saucepan of salted water. Bring to the boil and cook for about 10 minutes, or until tender. Drain the potatoes and allow them to steam dry for about 5 minutes, then tip them back into the pan. Mash the potatoes with the butter and the reserved poaching milk.

Flake the haddock into the mash along with half of the parsley, the zest of 1 lemon, the mustards, Cheddar, Worcestershire sauce, white pepper and a good pinch of salt. Mix everything together. Divide the mixture into eight and shape into patties, each weighing about 150g (5½oz). Place the patties onto a tray or plate lined with nonstick baking paper. Cover and place in the fridge to firm up.

Place the flour in a large shallow dish with a pinch each of salt and pepper. Place the beaten eggs in another shallow dish. Mix the breadcrumbs and remaining parsley in a third shallow dish. Remove the patties from the fridge. One at a time, dust the patties in the seasoned flour, dip in the beaten egg and roll in the breadcrumbs. Return each patty to the tray.

Heat the olive oil in a frying pan on a medium heat and cook the fishcakes in two batches for about 7 minutes on each side, or until golden and cooked through.

Remove the fishcakes from the pan and serve immediately with the remaining lemon cut into wedges.

If samphire is in season, it's lovely on the side – just add to a pan of boiling water for a few minutes, then toss with butter. Otherwise, Tenderstem broccolli or spring greens are perfect. Some English mustard or horseradish cream is another nice touch.

Red Lentil and Mixed Bean Casserole

PREP: 20 MINUTES · COOK: 1 HOUR 35 MINUTES · SERVES 6–8

1 red pepper, cored, deseeded
    and sliced

1 yellow pepper, cored, deseeded
    and sliced

2 red onions, finely sliced

200g (7oz) chestnut mushrooms,
    trimmed and sliced

3 garlic cloves, crushed

2 tablespoons rapeseed oil

1 tablespoon dried oregano

1 tablespoon dried basil

1 teaspoon sweet smoked paprika

1 tablespoon smoked chilli harissa
    paste (optional)

2 tablespoons tomato purée

2 × 400g (14oz) cans chopped
    tomatoes

100g (3½oz) dried red lentils

1 × 400g (14oz) can mixed beans,
    drained

150g (5½oz) fine green beans,
    trimmed and sliced

100g (3½oz) baby spinach leaves

salt and pepper

A super-satisfying, one-pot vegetable stew, packed with good stuff. Our recipe has been the same since the very early days, which tells you everything you need to know. If you're planning to freeze this dish, don't add the green beans and spinach until you are reheating in the oven.

Preheat the oven to 200°C fan/220°C/425°F/Gas Mark 7.

Place the peppers, onions, mushrooms and garlic in a large, ovenproof casserole dish. Toss with the oil, oregano, basil, paprika and smoked chilli harrisa paste (if using), and season well. Cover the pan with a lid, then bake in the oven for 30 minutes, stirring halfway through, until the vegetables are softened and starting to colour.

When the vegetables are ready, add the tomato purée, chopped tomatoes, lentils, mixed beans and green beans, along with 200ml (7fl oz) water. Stir well to combine. Again, cover the pan with a lid and return to the oven for 1 hour, or until bubbling and thickened. When you're nearly ready to serve, stir in the spinach and return the pan to the oven for 3–5 minutes. Remove from the oven, season to taste and serve.

This is great served on jacket potatoes or with mash. Or opt for garlic bread and a salad. You can add other flourishes, too – crack in some eggs at the end (one per person should do it) and return to the oven until they are cooked, ripple through spoonfuls of plain or coconut yoghurt, or crumble some feta cheese on top...

Vegetable Moussaka

PREP: 20 MINUTES · COOK: 1 HOUR 45 MINUTES · SERVES 4

2 large Maris Piper potatoes, peeled

5 tablespoons rapeseed oil, plus extra
for greasing

2 onions, finely diced

3 garlic cloves, crushed

2 teaspoons ground cinnamon

1 teaspoon dried mint

1½ tablespoons dried oregano

2 tablespoons tomato purée

250ml (9fl oz) Italian red wine

1 × 400g (14oz) can chopped tomatoes

400ml (14fl oz) vegetable stock

100g (3½oz) dried red lentils

1 aubergine, sliced into 1cm
(½ inch) rounds

250g (9oz) ricotta cheese

200g (7oz) feta cheese, crumbled

100ml (3½fl oz) milk

a little grated nutmeg

40g (1½oz) fresh breadcrumbs

salt and pepper

*Greek salad is the only thing to serve
with this. We use this recipe from
our Greek friend Penny: Mix 350g
(12oz) tomatoes, sliced or quartered,
⅓ onion, diced, 1 green pepper, diced,
and ½ cucumber, diced, with 150g
(5½oz) feta cheese, 50g (1¾oz) olives,
2 tablespoons of dried oregano and
maybe 1 tablespoon of capers as well.
Make a dressing with 6–8 tablespoons
olive oil, 2 tablespoons white wine
vinegar and seasoning. Let everything
soak in the dressing, then dip fresh
bread in the juice at the bottom of
the bowl – this is called a 'papara'.*

Sensationally flavourful lentils beneath layers of griddled aubergines and
soft potatoes. We've used a cheat's béchamel sauce here to save time and
because the mix of ricotta and feta is absolutely divine (we make a classic,
roux-based sauce when we cook this recipe in our kitchen).

Place the whole potatoes in a small saucepan of water. Bring to the boil and
cook for 10–12 minutes, or until the potatoes are cooked through but not mushy.
Drain and allow to steam dry until cool enough to handle.

Meanwhile, place a large saucepan on a medium heat. Add 2 tablespoons of
the oil followed by the onions, garlic, cinnamon, mint and 1 tablespoon of the
oregano. Cook for about 10 minutes, or until softened.

Stir in the tomato purée and wine. Reduce the wine by half, then add the
chopped tomatoes, stock and lentils. Bring to the boil, reduce the heat and allow
to simmer for 30 minutes, stirring occasionally, or until the lentils are cooked
and the sauce reduced. Season to taste.

Place a griddle pan or large frying pan on a medium heat. Brush the aubergine
slices with oil and griddle or fry for about 4 minutes on each side. You will need to
do this in batches. Transfer the cooked aubergine to a plate and place to one side.

Meanwhile, place the ricotta and half of the feta in a bowl with the milk and a few
gratings of nutmeg. Season and mix well to a thick sauce consistency, then place
to one side.

Place the breadcrumbs in a bowl, mix with the remaining oil and season. Slice
the now cooled potatoes into 1cm (½ inch) thick slices.

Preheat the oven to 180°C fan/200°C/400°F/Gas Mark 6. Grease a 30 × 20cm
(12 × 8 inch) ovenproof dish.

Spoon the lentil sauce into the dish and top with slices of aubergine and potato,
alternating them as you go, so they slightly overlap. Spoon the cheese sauce
over, crumble over the remaining feta and sprinkle with the breadcrumb mix.

Bake in the oven for 30 minutes, or until golden and bubbling. Allow to sit for
5 minutes before serving.

A FREEZER FULL OF JOY

Or, how to fall in love with your freezer... It will come as no surprise that we love our freezers at COOK. Freezing provides us with a natural way to preserve food, reduce waste and save both time and money. With a little bit of know-how, hardly any of the ingredients in your fridge should ever end up in the bin. Here are our top tips for getting the most out of your freezer.

Veg about to turn?

Peppers, onions, courgettes, tomatoes and mushrooms all have a tendency to lie forgotten in the veg drawer of your fridge. Dice or slice roughly, pop onto a baking tray, season, drizzle with oil and roast at 180°C fan/200°C/400°F/ Gas Mark 6 for 20–30 minutes. Leave to cool, then freeze. To reheat, just empty onto a baking tray and cook in a preheated oven (as above) until they start to sizzle. You could add them straight to a sauce to heat through, too.

Root ginger

This keeps for months frozen. Cut a big root into smaller pieces for ease of use. Peel with a teaspoon and grate while still frozen.

Ice and a slice

Cut up lemons and limes and keep them frozen to pop straight into your G&T. That half-drunk bottle of wine beginning to turn that you're about to pour down the sink? STOP. Pour it into ice-cube trays and freeze to add to sauces or gravy. Decent vodka should, of course, always be kept in the freezer, too.

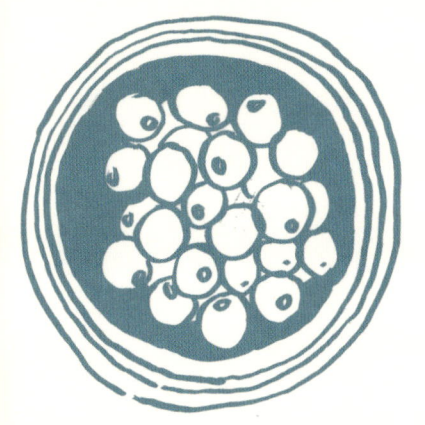

Raw veg

Ideally, you would blanch veg before freezing it – this means cooking very briefly in boiling water in order to preserve flavour, texture and colour. Immerse the veg in a large pan of boiling water for 1–2 minutes until just slightly softened, then immediately drain and plunge into a large bowl of freezing cold water. Drain and dry on a piece of kitchen paper before freezing. But, let's be honest, if you're in a rush, then you really just want to peel, chop and freeze. In the main, if you're going to end up cooking the veg, this will be absolutely fine. Here's a brief guide to help you decide whether you can freeze your veg as they are or not:

- **Yes (blanched is best but raw is fine)** – Peeled and sliced broccoli, peppers, carrots, runner beans, parsnips, cabbage, kale, butternut squash and fennel.
- **Yes (raw)** – Diced onion and leek.
- **No (do not freeze)** – Generally anything that's best enjoyed crisp and/or has a high water content, like celery, cucumber, lettuce, radishes, bean sprouts, courgettes, aubergines, mushrooms and tomatoes.

Fruit

With a lot of fruit, the flavour preserves well but not the texture (fruit is around 95 per cent water and goes mushy when frozen). Of course, this doesn't matter a jot for smoothies, coulis and, most importantly, margaritas – frozen fruit straight from the freezer can replace the ice. As with veg, it is best to blanch fruit before freezing it, although freezing raw is fine, too. Conveniently, you can freeze whole bananas in their skins – again, great for smoothies. Apples and pears can be peeled, sliced, tossed in lemon or lime juice (to help retain their colour), frozen in plastic bags and used in pies or crumbles. Alternatively, stew apples, pears, apricots or plums with sugar, freeze, then use to top porridge or muesli.

Roasties

If you're cooking roast potatoes on a Sunday, double up the amount to freeze some for another day. Follow the normal routine: parboil in salted water until almost cooked (6–10 minutes depending on size), drain, then fluff up the outsides by tossing them around in the pan or colander. Transfer the ones you're freezing into a container large enough for you to arrange them in a single layer. Leave to cool, drizzle with some oil and freeze. To cook, pop them onto a roasting tray straight from the freezer, add some more oil and put in the oven at 180°C fan/200°C/400°F/ Gas Mark 6 for 40–50 minutes. Job done.

Milk

Milk in unopened cartons can be frozen (for about 1 month) as long as there is a gap between the milk and the lid – all liquids expand as they freeze; if there isn't enough room, the lid might pop off or the carton could split. Defrost in the fridge and shake well before using. Butter is also fine to freeze for a few months, but cheese is a bit more complicated. Hard cheeses (such as Cheddar, Parmesan or firm blues) can generally handle freezing well – in fact, grated cheese can be frozen for up to 4 months and used straight from the freezer. For soft cheeses (such as Brie or Camembert), it's another story – the high water content creates a weird texture when the cheese is defrosted (not weird and wonderful, just plain weird). If you're going to cook the cheese, however, then this isn't an issue – we sell a frozen Camembert for baking, for example. You can also use softer cheeses to make a sauce that you then freeze. Yoghurt and cream can be frozen but will need a good stir once defrosted, as foods with higher fat contents tend to separate when frozen.

Cakes and bakes

Sugar is your friend! It helps maintain the texture of cakes in the freezer but, be careful, it can also pick up other aromas, so make sure baked cakes are tightly sealed in their containers.

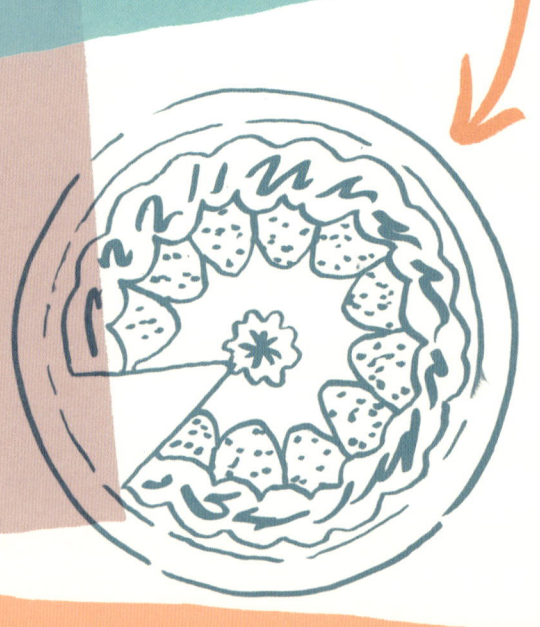

Fish

Can fish be successfully frozen? Well, this depends on the catch of the day... Lean fish (cod, haddock, hake, plaice and sole) can be kept frozen for about 6 months. On the other hand, fatty fish (salmon, mackerel and tuna) can only be kept frozen for 2 months. Again, make sure the fish is vacuum-sealed, as any air that gets in will destroy it.

Poultry

You don't ever want to fall fowl (sorry!) of a piece of chicken or turkey that has gone bad, so make sure you label poultry clearly. A tightly wrapped whole chicken will last for 1 year in the freezer. Turkey will be good for 7 months and duck, with its high fat content, 6 months. Individual poultry parts (thighs, wings, breasts, and so on) can stay in your freezer for 9 months. However, you will need to use any cooked poultry from your freezer within 6 months.

Meat

Fresh meat is generally fine to freeze, especially if you're going to use it for curries or stews. Where the sauce is the main flavour, it's almost impossible to detect if the beef or chicken breasts used were frozen. Just make sure that the meat is vacuum-sealed, so that it is protected from freezer burn.

A final word...

The most adaptable meals are the most useful to have in the freezer. Our holy trinity would be:

- **Bolognese** (see the ragu recipe in Lasagne al Forno on page 56). Turn it into a spaghetti Bolognese, a chilli, a cottage pie or, of course, everyone's favourite, a lasagne.
- **Chicken casserole** (see our Hearty Chicken Casserole on page 91). Make this into a pie with pastry or potato on top, or serve it with pasta, potatoes or rice.
- **Veggie casserole** (see our Red Lentil and Mixed Bean Casserole on page 75). Go Greek by adding green olives, capers and halloumi; give it a Spanish twist by adding butter beans, paprika and cumin; serve with sourdough garlic bread; or top with filo pastry for a crisp and golden pie.

'People who love
to eat are always
the best people'
— Julia Child

KITCHEN WISDOM NO.3

Relax, It's the Weekend

You made it! Your reward? More time at the table with the people you love.

Recipes to kick back and relax with.

Beef Bourguignon

PREP: 20 MINUTES, PLUS MARINATING · COOK: 3 HOURS 40 MINUTES · SERVES 6–8

FOR THE BEEF AND MARINADE

1kg (2lb 4oz) top rump beef (or stewing beef), diced into 3cm (1¼ inch) pieces

4 bay leaves

4 thyme sprigs

4 rosemary sprigs

700ml (1¼ pints) red wine, preferably a Merlot

FOR THE SAUCE

6 tablespoons rapeseed oil

2 onions, finely sliced

4 garlic cloves, finely chopped

2 tablespoons plain flour

500ml (18fl oz) good-quality beef stock

1 tablespoon redcurrant jelly

1 tablespoon tomato purée

200g (7oz) smoked back bacon, sliced

175g (6oz) shallots, quartered, or 30 silverskin onions

300g (10½oz) chestnut mushrooms, trimmed and sliced

30ml (2 tablespoons) balsamic vinegar

1 tablespoon demerara sugar

salt and pepper

2 tablespoons finely chopped flat leaf parsley, to garnish

Mashed potato is our go-to companion for this dish. Liven it up by stirring through a couple of spoonfuls of horseradish. For veg, try Braised Red Cabbage or Creamed Spinach (see page 179) or some kale or broccoli, sautéed with garlic and butter.

Time is the essential ingredient for a great Beef Bourguignon. In our kitchen we braise the beef for hours, so it's meltingly tender and flavourful. At home, the long, slow oven cook breaks up the hands-on work, so everything feels more relaxed and your kitchen smells divine. Drinking red wine during this period is definitely allowed. If you're freezing this dish, cool and freeze it after the long cooking time, before you add the bacon, shallots (or silverskin onions) and mushrooms. Defrost, then add these and pick up the recipe at the final cooking stage.

A few hours before you are ready to cook – preferably the night before – place the beef into a large bowl or container with a lid. Add the bay leaves and thyme and rosemary sprigs, pour over the wine and stir, so the beef is well coated. Place the lid on and put in the fridge to allow the flavours to infuse the beef.

When ready to cook, preheat the oven to 180°C fan/200°C/400°F/Gas Mark 6. Place a large, lidded casserole dish on a medium heat and add 2 tablespoons of the oil. Remove the beef from the marinade using a slotted spoon (keeping the marinade) and cook the beef, in batches, for about 10 minutes until brown all over, then transfer to a dish to one side. Repeat the process until all the beef is browned.

Add 2 more tablespoons of the oil to the pan and add the onions. Fry for 5 minutes, or until translucent, then add the garlic and fry for a further 5 minutes. Add the flour and cook, stirring, for 2 minutes. Add a good splash of the beef marinade and scrape all the bits from the bottom of the pan using a wooden spoon. Add the rest of the marinade along with the beef stock, redcurrant jelly and tomato purée. Simmer, stirring well, for 2 minutes. Add the browned beef and bring to the boil. Cover and cook in the oven for about 3 hours, or until the sauce has thickened a little and the meat is tender.

After 2½ hours, place a large nonstick frying pan on a medium heat. Add the remaining oil and the bacon. Fry for a few minutes, stirring well, until golden. Add the shallots or silverskin onions and the mushrooms. Cook for a further 5–10 minutes, or until everything is lightly golden. Add the balsamic vinegar and sugar. Stir until the sugar has dissolved. Carefully add the contents of the pan to the casserole dish. Stir to combine, then return the pan to the oven, uncovered, for the last 20 minutes of cooking time, or until the sauce is bubbling and the onions have softened. Check occasionally – if the sauce gets too thick, add a splash of water.

Season to taste, then serve with the parsley sprinkled on top.

Chilli, Ginger and Soy Slow-roasted Pork Belly with Spicy Tomato Chutney

PREP: 15 MINUTES, PLUS MARINATING · COOK: 3 HOURS 30 MINUTES · SERVES 6

FOR THE PORK AND MARINADE

1 tablespoon chilli flakes

1 thumb-sized piece of fresh root ginger, peeled and grated

4 garlic cloves, crushed

100ml (3½fl oz) light soy sauce

100ml (3½fl oz) clear honey

grated zest and juice of 3 limes

1 teaspoon freshly ground black pepper

1.5–2kg (3lb 5oz–4lb 8oz) pork belly, skin scored

salt

FOR THE TOMATO CHUTNEY

1 tablespoon cumin seeds

1 tablespoon coriander seeds

½ tablespoon black peppercorns

1 tablespoon olive oil

2 onions, finely chopped

4 garlic cloves, finely chopped

1 thumb-sized piece of fresh root ginger, peeled and grated

½ teaspoon chilli flakes

100ml (3½fl oz) white wine vinegar

50g (1¾oz) soft light brown sugar

1 tablespoon fish sauce

750g (1lb 10oz) cherry tomatoes, quartered

The Vietnamese banh mi is possibly the best sandwich in the world (discuss) and was the inspiration for this slow-roasted pork belly, bathed in classic Asian flavours and married to a rich, jammy tomato chutney. It only featured on our menu for a couple of years, sadly, so it's great to revive the recipe here.

Choose an ovenproof dish that will be a snug fit for the piece of pork belly. Add all the marinade ingredients to the dish and whisk to combine. Place the pork on top, skin-side up, and sprinkle a good pinch of salt all over the skin. Try not to get any marinade on the skin, to ensure good crackling. Cover loosely and place in the fridge overnight, or for at least 4 hours.

When you're ready to cook the pork, preheat the oven to 130°C fan/150°C/ 300°F/Gas Mark 2.

Place the dish containing the pork in the oven and cook for 3 hours. After this time, increase the oven temperature to 220°C fan/240°C/475°F/Gas Mark 9. Allow the pork belly skin to crackle and crisp up for about 20 minutes, keeping an eye on it to make sure it doesn't burn.

Meanwhile, make the tomato chutney. Place a medium saucepan on a medium heat. Add the cumin seeds, coriander seeds and peppercorns to the dry pan and cook for 2 minutes, or until toasted and smelling delicious. Transfer to a bowl and place to one side. Return the pan to the heat and add the oil, followed by the onions, garlic and ginger. Cook for about 10 minutes, or until the onions turn translucent. Add the remaining ingredients along with the toasted spices. Turn up the heat, bring to the boil, then reduce the heat to low and cook for about 30 minutes, stirring occasionally, until the mixture is jammy and delicious. Transfer to a bowl and allow to cool.

Remove the pork from the oven and allow to rest for 10 minutes. Carve into strips and serve alongside the tomato chutney.

Serve with a crunchy, punchy salad: shred ¼ crunchy cabbage and mix with 2 grated carrots, 1 sliced apple and a few sprigs of chopped mint. Make a dressing with 1 tablespoon soy sauce, 2 tablespoons toasted sesame oil, 1 tablespoon clear honey, the juice of 1 lime and a splash of fish sauce.

Pork Dijon with Pink Pickled Onions

PREP: 15 MINUTES · COOK: 1 HOUR 15 MINUTES · SERVES 4

FOR THE PINK PICKLED ONIONS
200ml (7fl oz) red wine vinegar
pinch of salt
pinch of caster sugar
1 red onion, finely sliced

FOR THE PORK DIJON
60ml (4 tablespoons) rapeseed oil
350g (12oz) chestnut mushrooms,
　　trimmed and sliced
600g (1lb 5oz) pork tenderloin,
　　cut into 1cm (½ inch) strips
3 onions, finely sliced
30ml (2 tablespoons) balsamic vinegar
100ml (3½fl oz) dry sherry
300ml (10fl oz) white wine
juice of 1 lemon
30g (1oz) butter
30g (1oz) plain flour
150ml (5fl oz) milk
½ teaspoon ground white pepper
400ml (14fl oz) chicken stock
100ml (3½fl oz) crème fraîche
1 tablespoon wholegrain mustard
1 teaspoon English mustard
1 tablespoon Dijon mustard
2 tablespoons chopped fresh chives
salt and pepper
2 tablespoons chopped flat leaf parsley,
　　to garnish

COOK founder Ed's favourite dish and a must for mustard lovers. The beautiful, creamy sauce balances out the tartness of the mustards and the pink, quick-pickled onions. We suggest using a pork tenderloin, but you can also use leg steaks, sliced into strips.

First, make the pink pickled onions. Place the vinegar, salt and sugar in a small saucepan over a medium heat. Bring to the boil, then add the red onion. Reduce to a simmer and cook for about 5 minutes until the vinegar starts to evaporate and the onions soften. Drain the onions and transfer to a bowl to one side.

To cook the pork, place a large nonstick frying pan on a medium heat. Add half of the oil, then fry the mushrooms and pork in batches for 5–10 minutes until the mushrooms are golden. Transfer each batch to a large bowl to one side.

Keep the frying pan on the heat and add the remaining oil. Add the onions and cook until they are starting to soften but are not browned. Add the vinegar, sherry, wine and lemon juice. Stir well. Bring to the boil, then reduce to a simmer for 10–15 minutes, or until the liquid has reduced by half. Return the pork and mushrooms to the pan. Add the butter and flour, and cook, stirring, for a few minutes until thickened, then stir in the milk. Add the white pepper and chicken stock. Stir well, then reduce the heat to a simmer and cook for 20 minutes, or until the pork is tender.

Add the crème fraîche, mustards and chives, and stir. The sauce may look a little split for a moment but it will come back together once everything is well combined. Season to taste and remove from the heat. Divide between individual dishes, sprinkle the chopped parsley on top and spoon over the pink pickled onions.

It may be a geographical aberration, but this goes surprisingly well with pasta, especially thick-ribboned pappardelle or big rigatoni tubes. Less controversial accompaniments are rice or mashed potato.

Hearty Chicken Casserole

PREP: 15 MINUTES · COOK: 1 HOUR 55 MINUTES · SERVES 4

8 bone-in, skin-on chicken thighs
   and drumsticks, total weight
   about 1kg (2lb 4oz)
3 tablespoons rapeseed oil
2 leeks, sliced
1 onion, chopped
2 garlic cloves, crushed
2 carrots, sliced
500g (1lb 2oz) swede, diced
splash of white wine (optional)
2 tablespoons picked thyme
2 tablespoons tomato purée
700ml (1¼ pints) chicken stock
1 × 400g (14oz) can chopped tomatoes
1 tablespoon wholegrain mustard
salt and pepper
2 tablespoons chopped flat leaf
   parsley, to garnish

Hearty by name, hearty by nature. A simple and satisfying pot of slow-cooked chicken and chunky veg. A warm hug of a meal on a cold and gloomy weekend.

Season the chicken all over with salt and pepper. Place a large lidded casserole dish on a medium heat. Add the oil, followed by the chicken, skin-side down, and cook for 10 minutes until brown all over. You will need to do this in two batches. Remove the chicken from the heat, transfer to a plate and place to one side.

Preheat the oven to 180°C fan/200°C/400°F/Gas Mark 6.

Place the casserole dish back on the heat. Add the leeks, onion and garlic to the pan. Cook for about 10 minutes, or until the onions are translucent. Add the carrots and swede, and fry for 5 minutes, then add the wine (if using) and allow to bubble and deglaze the dish for a few seconds. Add the thyme and tomato purée, and stir to coat. Add the stock, chopped tomatoes and mustard. Stir well, then nestle the chicken back into the pan. Cover and cook in the oven for 1 hour, or until the chicken is cooked and tender.

After this cooking time, remove the lid and increase the oven temperature to 200°C fan/220°C/425°F/Gas Mark 7. Cook the casserole for a further 20 minutes to thicken the sauce a little more.

Remove the pan from the oven, season to taste and divide the casserole between individual dishes. Scatter the chopped parsley on top and serve.

Nothing fancy needed here, just some mashed potato or you could even do pasta. Or, to make life easy, you can add halved new potatoes to the casserole dish – about 500g (1lb 2oz) should be plenty – before it goes in the oven for the second time (check they're done before serving). Some warm crusty bread, topped with melting butter, never goes amiss either.

Jerk-seasoned Chicken with Pineapple Salsa

PREP: 20 MINUTES · COOK: 1 HOUR 20 MINUTES · SERVES 4

FOR THE JERK-SEASONED CHICKEN

3 tablespoons jerk paste

3 tablespoons rapeseed oil

8 boneless chicken thighs, skin on, about 70g (2½oz) each

1 onion, thinly sliced

3 garlic cloves, crushed

1 red chilli, deseeded and finely chopped

1 teaspoon ground turmeric

1 teaspoon ground cumin

1 teaspoon ground coriander

1 teaspoon ground allspice

1 teaspoon ground cinnamon

2 tablespoons tomato purée

1 × 400ml (14fl oz) can coconut milk

salt and pepper

FOR THE PINEAPPLE SALSA

125g (4½oz) pineapple, peeled, cored and cut into 1cm (½ inch) chunks

200g (7oz) roasted red peppers, chopped into 1cm (½ inch) pieces

30g (1oz) fresh coriander, chopped

4 spring onions, finely sliced

finely grated zest and juice of 1 lime, plus extra lime wedges to garnish

salt and pepper

A burst of spicy-and-sweet Caribbean flavours to brighten any weekend, inspired by a one-pot meal we make. The zesty salsa is a lovely salve after a mouthful of heat. If you like things milder, just tone down the chilli.

Preheat the oven to 180°C fan/200°C/400°F/Gas Mark 6.

Mix the jerk paste and 2 tablespoons of the oil in a large bowl and place to one side. Place a large ovenproof casserole dish on a medium heat. In batches, place the chicken thighs, skin-side down, in the dish and cook for 5–10 minutes until the skin crisps and colours, then transfer the chicken to the bowl of jerk paste. Repeat with the remaining chicken thighs. When all the chicken is cooked, rub the jerk seasoning paste over the chicken (you might want to use gloves for this as the paste is spicy and it can get a little messy).

In the same casserole dish, add the remaining oil with the onion, garlic and chilli. Cook on a low heat, stirring all the time, for about 5 minutes, or until the onion is translucent. Add the spices and cook for a further 5 minutes while stirring.

Stir in the tomato purée, then add the coconut milk to the pan. Swill out the can with a little water and add that to the dish, too. Bring to the boil, then reduce to a simmer for 5 minutes. Stir well, then return the chicken to the casserole dish. Cook in the oven, uncovered, for 40 minutes, or until the chicken is tender.

Meanwhile, combine all the salsa ingredients in a bowl, reserving a little of the coriander to garnish. Season to taste.

When the chicken is ready, remove from the oven and allow to stand for 5 minutes. Season to taste.

To serve, divide the chicken between plates, scatter over the reserved coriander and serve with the salsa, lime wedges and your choice of accompaniment.

Rice is the obvious choice to serve alongside. Soft flatbreads (see page 36) are another great option and are perfect for mopping up the sauce. Or make a burrito-style supper using tortilla wraps – shred the cooked chicken and mix with the sauce, heat some tortillas and let everybody help themselves from the casserole dish, with the bowl of salsa, a bowl of rice and some crisp salad, too.

Parmesan Chicken

PREP: 30 MINUTES · COOK: 1 HOUR 50 MINUTES · SERVES 4

FOR THE SAUCE

125ml (4fl oz) rapeseed oil

2 onions, chopped

2 garlic cloves, crushed

400g (14 oz) cherry tomatoes, halved

250g (9oz) roasted red peppers from
    a jar, drained and chopped

2 tablespoons tomato purée

1 teaspoon paprika

200ml (7fl oz) white wine

400ml (14fl oz) chicken stock

150ml (5fl oz) double cream

150g (5½oz) baby spinach

salt and pepper

FOR THE CHICKEN

100g (3½oz) plain flour

2 eggs, beaten

150g (5½oz) fresh breadcrumbs

3 tablespoons chopped flat leaf parsley

100g (3½oz) Parmesan cheese, grated

4 chicken breasts, total weight about
    600g (1lb 5oz)

salt and pepper

FOR THE POTATOES

1kg (2lb 4oz) new potatoes, halved

2 tablespoons chopped rosemary

A recent arrival on our menu and an instant hit. Crisply golden, Parmesan-crusted chicken breasts, with a creamy, fresh tomato sauce and roasted new potatoes. A dish full of sunshine, even when the sky isn't.

Place a large frying pan on a medium heat. Add 2 tablespoons of the oil, followed by the onions and garlic. Cook for 10 minutes, stirring occasionally, or until the onions are translucent. Add the tomatoes, peppers, tomato purée and paprika. Stir well. Increase the heat, add the white wine and reduce by half. Stir in the chicken stock, reduce to a simmer and cook for about 30 minutes until slightly thickened.

Meanwhile, coat the chicken. Place the flour on a plate and season. Place the beaten eggs in a large shallow dish. Place the breadcrumbs in another shallow dish and stir in most of the parsley and Parmesan, reserving a little of each. Working with one at a time, dust each chicken breast in the seasoned flour, then dip into the beaten egg, allowing the excess to drip off, and finally press each side of the chicken into the breadcrumbs. Carefully tap off the excess crumb and place onto a tray to one side.

Boil the potatoes for 10 minutes, drain and allow to steam dry for about 5 minutes.

Preheat the oven to 200°C fan/220°C/425°F/Gas Mark 7.

Place a large nonstick frying pan on a medium heat and add 4 tablespoons of the oil. Fry two chicken breasts at a time for 3 minutes on each side, or until the crumb is starting to look golden. Transfer the browned chicken to a large roasting tray and repeat with the remaining chicken, adding more oil when necessary. Add the potatoes to the tray with the chicken. Scatter over the rosemary and the reserved Parmesan. Season, then bake in the oven for 30–40 minutes.

When the chicken and potatoes are nearly ready, place the sauce back on a low heat. Stir in the cream and spinach. Allow the spinach to wilt and season the sauce to taste.

When the chicken is ready, remove the roasting tray from the oven. Spoon the sauce onto individual plates and top with the chicken and potatoes. Scatter over the reserved parsley and serve.

Beef Stroganoff

PREP: 20 MINUTES · COOK: 40–45 MINUTES · SERVES 4

2 tablespoons plain flour

400g (14oz) sirloin (trimmed of fat)
    or fillet steak, cut into 1.5–2cm
    (⅝–¾ inch) thick strips

3 tablespoons rapeseed oil

2 onions, finely sliced

2 garlic cloves, sliced

1 tablespoon picked thyme

250g (9oz) chestnut mushrooms,
    trimmed and sliced

1 teaspoon paprika

40g (1½oz) unsalted butter

100ml (3½fl oz) dry sherry or brandy

150ml (5fl oz) beef stock

100ml (3½fl oz) single cream

squeeze of lemon juice

salt and pepper

TO GARNISH

2 tablespoons chopped flat leaf parsley

4 small gherkins, finely chopped

Pretty much anything goes when choosing what to serve this with – rice, pasta (go with thick ribbons of pappardelle), mashed potato, crusty bread, chips... You can dress it up or down. Add seasonal greens or a green salad on the side, if you like.

The Great Taste judges praised this dish for its 'lovely, creamy and boozy sauce' when they gave us an award one year. It's an excellent way to make a piece of steak go a bit further. You can also serve individual steaks and make the stroganoff as a sauce. You can even make it meat-free – triple the amount of mushrooms (and maybe use a few different varieties) and switch in vegetable stock for beef stock.

Tip the flour into a large bowl, season well, then add the steak. Toss to coat, then place to one side.

Place a large nonstick frying pan or large shallow casserole pan on a medium–high heat. Add 2 tablespoons of the oil, then the steak – you might need to do this in two batches. Fry for 3–5 minutes until the pieces of meat are browned but still pink in the middle. Transfer the steak to a clean dish and place to one side.

Return the pan to the heat and add the remaining oil. Add the onions, garlic and thyme. Cook for 10 minutes, or until the onions are translucent. Add the mushrooms and half of the paprika. Fry for 5–10 minutes, stirring well, until the mushrooms are browned. Add the butter and allow to sizzle, then add the sherry or brandy and cook until reduced by half. Scrape off any delicious brown bits from the bottom of the pan with a wooden spoon and stir into the sauce.

Add the stock, simmer for 10 minutes to reduce by about one-third, then lower the heat and stir in the cream and a squeeze of lemon juice. Season to taste. Return the steak to the pan and stir well.

Divide the beef between individual dishes to serve, then spoon over the sauce. Sprinkle with the chopped parsley and remaining paprika, and top with the chopped gherkins.

Salmon Rarebit with Roasted Grape, Walnut and Chicory Salad

PREP: 25 MINUTES · COOK: 35–40 MINUTES · SERVES 6–8

35g (1¼oz) unsalted butter

30g (1oz) plain flour

100ml (3½fl oz) stout or ale,
   at room temperature

50ml (2fl oz) crème fraîche

½ teaspoon English mustard

1 teaspoon Worcestershire sauce

100g (3½oz) mature Cheddar
   cheese, grated

1 egg yolk

70g (2½oz) baby spinach

800g–1kg (1lb 12oz–2lb 4oz) side
   of salmon, skin on

50g (1¾oz) sun-dried tomatoes,
   chopped

FOR THE TOPPING

1 slice day-old bread

grated zest of 1 lemon

1 tablespoon chopped flat leaf parsley

1 tablespoon chopped chives

2 tablespoons grated Parmesan cheese

1 tablespoon rapeseed oil

FOR THE SALAD

250g (9oz) seedless red grapes,
   removed from their stalks

100g (3½oz) walnut halves

2 tablespoons chopped tarragon

3 heads of chicory, leaves separated
   and sliced

1 teaspoon English mustard

2 tablespoons white wine vinegar

5 tablespoons rapeseed oil

1 teaspoon clear honey

salt and pepper

This dish came about when we were working on a Welsh rarebit-topped starter dish for Christmas. We happened to have some salmon around and thought we'd experiment. Hold onto your oven mitts, we might just have something here! There's a bit of a thermidor vibe with the rich, creamy rarebit sauce on top of the sweet-fleshed seafood. It's properly indulgent. While we suggest using a side of salmon, you can, of course, use individual salmon fillets instead – just take 5–10 minutes off the cooking time.

Preheat the oven to 180°C fan/200°C/400°F/Gas Mark 6. Place a medium saucepan on a low heat and add 30g (1oz) of the butter. Allow it to melt, then stir in the flour. Cook, still stirring, for 2 minutes, or until the paste starts to bubble. Gradually whisk in the stout or ale and cook for 3 minutes until thick and smooth. Whisk in the crème fraîche, mustard, Worcestershire sauce, cheese and egg yolk until smooth, then place to one side.

Place a frying pan on a medium heat and add the remaining butter. Once melted, add the spinach and stir well for 2 minutes, or until wilted. Remove from the heat and tip into a colander. When cool enough to handle, place the spinach in a clean tea towel and squeeze the liquid out. Chop the spinach and fold into the sauce.

To make the topping, place the bread in a food processor and blitz to a rough crumb. Transfer to a bowl and mix with the remaining topping ingredients and a good pinch each of salt and pepper.

Line a large roasting tray with nonstick baking paper. Place the salmon, skin-side down, on the tray. Spoon the sauce over the salmon, scatter over the sun-dried tomatoes and sprinkle over the topping. Cook in the oven for 25–30 minutes, or until the salmon is tender and the crumb is golden. Meanwhile, place the grapes and walnuts on a baking tray and cook in the oven for 20 minutes, or until the grapes are jammy and the walnuts toasted.

Meanwhile, make the salad. Place the tarragon and chicory in a large salad bowl. In a small bowl, make a dressing by whisking the mustard, vinegar, oil and honey with a pinch each of salt and pepper. When the grapes, walnuts and salmon are ready, remove them from the oven and allow the salmon to sit for 5 minutes. Add the grapes and walnuts to the salad bowl and toss with the dressing. Transfer the salmon to a serving platter and serve with the salad alongside.

Coq au Vin

PREP: 15 MINUTES, PLUS MARINATING · COOK: 2 HOURS 15 MINUTES · SERVES 4

FOR THE CHICKEN AND MARINADE

8 chicken thighs and drumsticks, skin on, total weight 1kg (2lb 4oz)

4 bay leaves

8 thyme sprigs

4 rosemary sprigs

4 garlic cloves, peeled and lightly crushed to hold shape but release the flavour

2 teaspoons whole black peppercorns

700ml (1¼ pints) full-bodied French red wine, preferably Burgundy

FOR THE SAUCE

60ml (4 tablespoons) rapeseed oil

100g (3½oz) smoked streaky bacon rashers, sliced into 1cm (½ inch) pieces

250g (9oz) chestnut mushrooms, trimmed and halved

100g (3½oz) shallots, cut into half moons, or 15 silverskin onions

3 tablespoons plain flour

50ml (2fl oz) brandy (optional)

200ml (7fl oz) good-quality chicken stock

2 teaspoons redcurrant jelly

1 tablespoon tomato purée

salt and pepper

2 tablespoons finely chopped flat leaf parsley, to garnish (optional)

Creamy mash is de rigueur, along with green beans, spinach or chard sautéed in butter and garlic.

Some reckon the history of this French classic goes back to Roman times. For us, it definitely goes back to the origins of COOK. Dale wanted to make it the traditional way: poaching whole chickens, using the stock in the sauce and portioning up the bird. He quickly realized the time and cost wouldn't be practical. But, to this day, we make sure the chicken is marinated for several hours and then use the wine to make the sauce.

A few hours before you are ready to cook – preferably the night before – prick the chicken pieces all over with a small sharp knife and place them in a large bowl or container with a lid. Add the bay leaves, thyme and rosemary sprigs, garlic cloves and peppercorns, pour over the wine and stir, so the chicken is well coated. Place the lid on and put in the fridge to marinate. When you're ready to cook, remove the chicken pieces from the marinade using a slotted spoon, pat dry with kitchen paper, transfer to a dish and place to one side. Keep the marinade.

Place a large, shallow, lidded casserole pan on a medium heat. When hot, add half of the oil and then half of the chicken pieces, skin-side down. Brown the chicken all over for about 2 minutes on each side, then transfer to a large dish and place to one side. Add the remaining oil to the pan, if you need to, and cook the remaining chicken pieces. Repeat the process until all the chicken has browned.

Preheat the oven to 160°C fan/180°C/350°F/Gas Mark 4.

Return the pan to a medium heat. Add the bacon and stir with a wooden spoon, scraping off any bits from the bottom of the pan. Once the bacon is cooked and golden, transfer it to the chicken dish. Add the mushrooms and shallots or silverskin onions to the pan and cook for 5–10 minutes, stirring well, until they become lightly golden. Add the flour and cook, stirring, for 2 minutes. Add the brandy (if using) and allow it to bubble, then add the marinade and reduce by one-third – this will take about 10 minutes. Add the stock and allow to reduce by one-third again – this will also take about 10 minutes. Stir in the redcurrant jelly and tomato purée. Return the chicken and bacon to the pan.

Cover the pan with a lid and cook in the oven for 1½ hours, or until the chicken is tender and cooked through. Remove the pan from the oven and season to taste.

Check the seasoning again before serving and remove the bay leaves and herb sprigs. Portion into individual dishes and sprinkle over the parsley (if using).

Cumin and Coriander-spiced Salmon with Crispy Bombay Aloo

PREP: 20 MINUTES, PLUS MARINATING · COOK: 1 HOUR 10 MINUTES · SERVES 4–6

FOR THE SALMON
800g–1kg (1lb 12oz–2lb 4oz)
    side of salmon, skin on
2 tablespoons cumin seeds
1 tablespoon coriander seeds
1 tablespoon garam masala
1 tablespoon light soft brown sugar
1 teaspoon sea salt
½ teaspoon ground black pepper
½ teaspoon chilli flakes
juice of 1 lime
3 garlic cloves, crushed
1 tablespoon rapeseed oil

FOR THE BOMBAY ALOO
AND SPICED TOMATOES
750g (1lb 10oz) new potatoes
3 tablespoons rapeseed oil
1 tablespoon cumin seeds
2 tablespoons dried curry leaves
1 teaspoon ground turmeric
1 tablespoon cornflour
1 onion, finely chopped
1 thumb-sized piece of fresh
    ginger, grated
2 garlic cloves, crushed
10g (¼oz) fresh coriander, leaves picked
    and chopped, stalks finely chopped
½ tablespoon black mustard seeds
1 teaspoon garam masala
2 tablespoons tomato purée
6 vine-ripened tomatoes, chopped
salt and pepper

Buttery, sweet salmon is a brilliant host for Indian spices and Bombay-style potatoes are the ideal accompaniment. If you prefer to use individual fillets rather than a whole side of salmon, reduce the cooking time by 5–10 minutes.

Preheat the oven to 180°C fan/200°C/400°F/Gas Mark 6. Line a large roasting tray with nonstick baking paper.

Place the salmon, skin-side down, on the prepared tray. In a bowl, mix the remaining salmon ingredients to make a paste and brush over the salmon. Cover with clingfilm and place in the fridge or a cool place to marinate while you prepare the potatoes.

Place the potatoes in a large saucepan of salted boiling water. Cook for 20 minutes, or until tender. Drain the potatoes in a colander, then return to the pan. Use a wooden spoon to crush the potatoes gently, while retaining their shape. Add 2 tablespoons of the oil, the cumin seeds, half of the curry leaves, the turmeric and a little salt and pepper. Toss well to coat the potatoes in the seasoning. Sprinkle over the cornflour and toss again. Take the salmon out of the fridge and remove the clingfilm. Arrange the potatoes around the salmon in the tray and roast in the oven for 20–25 minutes, or until the salmon is tender and cooked through and the potatoes have crisped up.

Meanwhile, place a medium frying pan on a medium heat. Add the remaining oil, followed by the onion, ginger, garlic and coriander stalks. Fry for 5 minutes, stirring, until the onion is starting to soften and look translucent. Add the remaining curry leaves, mustard seeds and garam masala and cook for 1 minute, stirring constantly. Add the tomato purée and cook, stirring well, for 1 minute. Add the chopped tomatoes, increase the heat and bring to the boil, then reduce to a simmer and cook for about 15 minutes, or until the tomatoes are softened but not cooked down. Season and remove from the heat.

When the salmon and potatoes are cooked, remove from the oven. If the potatoes need longer to crisp up, transfer the salmon to a platter and place the potatoes back in the oven for a further 10 minutes. Serve the salmon with the potatoes arranged around it, with the spiced tomatoes spooned over and the chopped coriander leaves scattered on top.

Salmon and Asparagus Gratin

PREP: 25 MINUTES · COOK: 1 HOUR · SERVES 4

30g (1oz) unsalted butter,
  plus extra for greasing

3 potatoes, total weight 500g
  (1lb 2oz), peeled

250g (9oz) asparagus, woody ends
  snapped off

1 onion, finely chopped

2 garlic cloves, sliced

2 tablespoons plain flour

100ml (3½fl oz) white wine

200ml (7fl oz) fish stock

100ml (3½fl oz) milk

150ml (5fl oz) double cream

100g (3½oz) mature Cheddar
  cheese, grated

4 tablespoons chopped flat leaf parsley

1 lemon, halved, plus extra lemon
  wedges to garnish

500g–600g (1lb 2oz–1lb 5oz)
  salmon fillet, skinned, deboned
  and chopped into chunks

2 tablespoons rapeseed oil

40g (1½oz) fresh breadcrumbs

salt and pepper

*Serve with a green salad in warmer
months and seasonal green veg the
rest of the year, with a knob of butter
swirled through. Grating some
lemon zest on the top really brings
the flavours to life.*

A true COOK original. A posh fish pie with a twist (the asparagus) and a satisfying, cheesy undertone. The asparagus season is disappointingly short, but broccoli florets make a good alternative. We tried reinventing this in 2012, using crushed baby potatoes on top, putting fennel in the sauce and removing the cheese ... disaster! We soon went back to the original recipe. We think of it as a mid-life crisis – if only they were all resolved so easily. If you're planning to freeze this, leave your potatoes and sauce to cool completely before assembling the dish, to ensure the fish doesn't overcook.

Grease a 30 × 20cm (12 × 8 inch) ovenproof dish with butter and place to one side.

Place the whole potatoes in a medium saucepan of water. Bring to the boil and cook for 10 minutes, or until just tender. For the last 3 minutes of cooking time, add the asparagus to the pan. Drain the potatoes and asparagus in a colander and allow to steam dry until cool enough to handle.

Place a medium saucepan on a low heat. Add the butter, allow it to melt, then add the onion and garlic. Cook until translucent, stirring occasionally. Add the flour and cook for 2 minutes. Add the white wine, increase the heat and cook, stirring, for about 10 minutes to reduce the liquid by three-quarters. Stir in the fish stock, milk and double cream, then stir in three-quarters of the cheese, 2 tablespoons of the parsley and a good squeeze of lemon juice. Season to taste, remove from the heat and place a lid on the pan.

Cut the potatoes into 1cm (½ inch) slices and the asparagus into 2cm (¾ inch) pieces, leaving the tips intact.

Preheat the oven to 180°C fan/200°C/400°F/Gas Mark 6.

Mix the salmon and asparagus into the sauce, then spoon into the prepared dish. Top with the slices of potato, drizzle over 1 tablespoon of the oil and season. In a small bowl, toss the breadcrumbs in the remaining oil, along with the remaining parsley and Cheddar. Season, then sprinkle the crumb topping over the potatoes. Bake in the oven for 25–30 minutes, or until golden and bubbling. Serve, garnished with lemon wedges, with your choice of accompaniment.

Roasted Tomato, Basil and Mozzarella Risotto

PREP: 15 MINUTES · COOK: 50 MINUTES · SERVES 6

300g (10½oz) cherry tomatoes, halved

3 tablespoons olive oil

1 litre (1¾ pints) vegetable stock

50g (1¾oz) unsalted butter

250g (9oz) shallots, finely chopped

3 garlic cloves, finely chopped

50g (1¾oz) basil, leaves picked and
    chopped, stalks chopped, plus extra
    leaves to garnish

30g (1oz) flat leaf parsley, leaves picked
    and chopped, stalks chopped

300g (10½oz) risotto rice

200ml (7fl oz) white wine

finely grated zest of 1 lemon

100g (3½oz) mascarpone cheese

125g (4½oz) ball of mozzarella
    cheese, torn

salt and pepper

TO GARNISH

50g (1¾oz) pine nuts, toasted

4 tablespoons basil pesto (optional)

You don't get anything more classically Italian than tomatoes, basil and mozzarella. Oh, hold on, you do if you make it a risotto. Roasting the tomatoes makes them lovely and sweet, while the mozzarella here is at its melted, stringy best.

Preheat the oven to 160°C fan/180°C/350°F/Gas Mark 4.

Place the cherry tomatoes in a small roasting tray with 1 tablespoon of the oil. Season and roast in the oven for 25 minutes, or until softened.

Meanwhile, heat the stock in a small saucepan on a low heat. Place a large, shallow, lidded casserole pan on a medium heat. Add the butter and remaining oil. Allow the butter to melt, then stir in the shallots, garlic, basil stalks and parsley stalks. Cook for about 10 minutes, stirring well, until the shallots are translucent.

Add the risotto rice and stir for 2 minutes to coat the rice – this starts the cooking process. Increase the heat, add the wine and allow to reduce by half. Reduce the heat to low and, ladle by ladle, stir in the hot stock, allowing the stock to soak into the rice with each addition. Keep stirring – why not have a glass of wine while you're standing at the hob stirring away?! After 25–30 minutes, the stock should be absorbed and the rice cooked, retaining a little bite.

Stir in a little lemon zest (reserving some to garnish), followed by the roasted tomatoes, mascarpone and mozzarella. Remove from the heat and cover. Allow the risotto to sit for 2 minutes.

When you're ready to serve, season the risotto to taste. Fold through the chopped basil and parsley leaves, and divide the risotto between individual dishes. Garnish with the remaining lemon zest, the pine nuts, basil leaves and a swirl of pesto, if you like.

A peppery rocket salad with a lemon and olive oil dressing provides a lovely contrast to the creamy risotto.

Vegetable and Chickpea Tagine

PREP: 20 MINUTES · COOK: 1 HOUR 30 MINUTES · SERVES 6–8

1 aubergine, chopped into 3cm
    (1¼ inch) chunks

1 yellow pepper, cored, deseeded and
    chopped into 3cm (1¼ inch) chunks

1 green pepper, cored, deseeded and
    chopped into 3cm (1¼ inch) chunks

2 red onions, sliced

3 garlic cloves, crushed

30g (1oz) fresh coriander, leaves picked
    and chopped, stalks chopped

30g (1oz) flat leaf parsley, leaves picked
    and chopped, stalks chopped

3 tablespoons rapeseed oil

1 tablespoon ground cinnamon

2 tablespoons ground cumin

1 tablespoon ground turmeric

2 tablespoons tomato purée

1 × 400g (14oz) can chopped tomatoes

1 × 400g (14oz) can chickpeas, drained

300ml (10fl oz) vegetable stock

4 dates, sliced

6 dried apricots, sliced

3 tablespoons flaked almonds

salt and pepper

A lovely, warming veggie casserole that's been on our menu for ages and is crazily good for you. Dates and apricots provide a sweet counterpoint to the dusky spices. If you'd like a bit more of a kick, add a spoonful of harissa paste or some dried chilli flakes.

Preheat the oven to 180°C fan/200°C/400°F/Gas Mark 6.

Place the aubergine, peppers, onions and garlic in a large ovenproof casserole dish or roasting tray. Add the coriander and parsley stalks, the oil and the spices. Season, toss together well and roast in the oven for about 30 minutes, turning halfway through the cooking time, or until the vegetables have softened but are still holding their shape.

When the vegetables are ready, add the tomato purée, chopped tomatoes, chickpeas, stock and dried fruit. Stir to combine.

Return the tagine to the oven for about 40 minutes, or until thickened. Sprinkle the almonds over the tagine and return to the oven for a further 20 minutes.

When the tagine is ready, remove from the oven and season to taste. Scatter over the chopped herb leaves and serve.

Couscous is the obvious choice of accompaniment. Mix through some pomegranate seeds, diced red onion and pistachios to bring it up a notch. Add natural or Greek yoghurt or crème fraîche for a cooling contrast, or you can crumble some feta on top. Warm flatbreads are always a good shout, too (see page 36). For more of a feast, serve it alongside our Griddled Vegetable Minted Couscous (see page 165) and Roasted Harissa Squash Salad with Preserved Lemon and Apricot Dressing (see page 175).

Moroccan-spiced Lamb Tagine

PREP: 5 MINUTES · COOK: 2 HOURS 50 MINUTES–3 HOURS 20 MINUTES · SERVES 4–6

4 tablespoons rapeseed oil

500g (1lb 2oz) lamb neck fillet
  or lamb shoulder, diced

2 onions, chopped

3 garlic cloves, chopped

1 tablespoon dried mint

½ teaspoon cayenne pepper

½ tablespoon ground coriander

½ tablespoon ground cumin

2 tablespoons ras-el-hanout

1 teaspoon sweet smoked paprika

2 black cardamom pods,
  lightly crushed (optional)

1 cinnamon stick

30g (1oz) fresh coriander, leaves picked
  and chopped, stalks chopped

3 bay leaves

3 tablespoons tomato purée

1 × 400g can chopped tomatoes

500ml (18fl oz) lamb stock

1 × 400g (14oz) can chickpeas, drained

8 dried prunes

2 tablespoons clear honey

50g (1¾oz) flaked almonds

salt and pepper

handful of pomegranate seeds
  to serve (optional)

Our iconic, award-winning recipe of meltingly tender, slow-cooked lamb in a sweet, fragrant sauce that's just the right kind of exotic. It's the perfect go-to when friends come round for dinner – make it ahead and then reheat to serve, so there's no rushing around the kitchen. We haven't counted, but we suspect this recipe has won more Great Taste awards than any other on our menu.

Place a large ovenproof casserole dish on a medium heat. Add the oil and brown the meat all over, in batches. Transfer to a plate and place to one side.

Return the dish to a medium–low heat and add the onions. Cook for 5 minutes until starting to soften, then increase the heat and add the garlic, mint, cayenne pepper, ground coriander, cumin, ras-el-hanout and paprika. Cook for 5 minutes, stirring occasionally, until the onions are softened and translucent. Add the cardamom pods (if using), cinnamon stick, coriander stalks and bay leaves. Stir in the tomato purée, chopped tomatoes, stock, chickpeas and prunes. Return the browned lamb to the dish and stir.

Preheat the oven to 160°C fan/180°C/350°F/Gas Mark 4.

Bring the tagine up to the boil, stir well, then reduce the heat to low. Place the lid on the pan and transfer to the oven for 2½–3 hours, or until the sauce has thickened and the meat is tender.

With about 20 minutes left of the cooking time, remove the lid to check the sauce. If it's very thick, add a splash of water, then add the honey, season to taste and scatter over the almonds. Return the tagine to the oven until the almonds are toasted.

Transfer the tagine to a serving dish, scatter over the pomegranate seeds and chopped coriander leaves, and serve.

Serve with couscous or rice, warm flatbreads (see page 36) cut into triangles, and yoghurt or crème fraîche with chopped mint stirred through. You could add a simple carrot and orange salad, too: 2–3 coarsely grated carrots and segments from 1 orange, cut in half, mixed with about 10g (¼oz) finely chopped fresh coriander and mint, and a dressing of 3 tablespoons olive oil, 2 tablespoons orange juice, 1 tablespoon brown sugar or maple syrup, and a little cumin and cinnamon to taste.

Quiche Lorraine

PREP: 50 MINUTES, PLUS CHILLING · COOK: 1 HOUR 30 MINUTES · SERVES 8–10

FOR THE FILLING

140g (5oz) semi-dried tomatoes in
    oil, plus 3 tablespoons of the oil
2 onions, finely chopped
4 egg yolks, plus 1 whole egg
250ml (9fl oz) double cream
100g (3½oz) mascarpone cheese
½ teaspoon ground white pepper
½ teaspoon sea salt
1 teaspoon dried basil
1 teaspoon dried parsley
100g (3½oz) cooked ham or
    gammon, chopped

FOR THE PASTRY

350g (12oz) plain flour, plus a little
    extra for dusting
½ teaspoon fine sea salt
180g (6¼oz) unsalted butter,
    chilled and cut into cubes,
    plus extra for greasing
2 teaspoons lemon juice
50ml (2fl oz) cold water
3 egg yolks

FOR THE TOPPING

125g (4½oz) mature Cheddar
    cheese, grated
1½ teaspoons chopped fresh chives

*Serve with a green salad with a
mustard dressing: 1 tablespoon Dijon
mustard, 2 tablespoons each olive oil
and white wine vinegar, and a pinch of
salt, all shaken together in a jam jar.*

For some reason, quiches are often reserved for special occasions or big gatherings. We're not sure why – especially given a quiche can last for a few days in the fridge and is delicious eaten both warm and cold.

Place a medium frying pan on a medium heat. Add 3 tablespoons of the oil from the semi-dried tomatoes to the pan. Add the onions and cook for 10 minutes until softened and turning golden. Transfer to a bowl to one side to cool.

To make the pastry, place the flour and salt in a large mixing bowl and stir to combine. Add the butter and rub in with your fingertips until the mixture resembles fine breadcrumbs. Make a well in the centre and add the lemon juice, then the measured water, a little bit at a time so the pastry doesn't get too wet, then the egg yolks. Use a dinner knife to incorporate the wet ingredients, then use your fingers to form the dough. Turn the dough out on a lightly floured surface and pat into a disc. Wrap the dough in clingfilm and place in the fridge for 30 minutes.

For the filling, whisk together the egg yolks, whole egg, double cream, mascarpone, pepper, salt, basil, parsley and half of the semi-dried tomatoes in a large bowl or jug. Cover and place in the fridge.

Lightly butter and flour a 27cm (10¾ inch) round, loose-bottomed tart tin. When the pastry has rested, roll it out on a clean, lightly floured work surface to 3mm (⅛ inch) thick. Line the tart tin with the pastry, allowing some to hang over the side – this can be trimmed before or after baking. Cover and return to the fridge for a further 30 minutes.

Preheat the oven to 170°C fan/190°C/375°F/Gas Mark 5. Remove the pastry case from the fridge. Prick the base all over with a fork. Line with nonstick baking paper and fill with baking beans. Blind bake in the oven for 20 minutes until cooked but not coloured. Remove the baking beans and return to the oven for a further 5–10 minutes until the base is cooked. Allow to cool a little on a wire rack. Reduce the oven temperature to 140°C fan/160°C/325°F/Gas Mark 3.

To assemble the quiche, spoon the onions into the pastry case along with the chopped ham or gammon. Pour over the creamy filling and top with the Cheddar, chives and the remaining semi-dried tomatoes. Cook in the oven for 40–50 minutes, or until just set. Allow to cool for at least 20 minutes before slicing and serving. Or chill completely in the fridge and serve cold.

Roasted Red Pepper and Goats' Cheese Quiche

PREP: 50 MINUTES, PLUS CHILLING · COOK: 1 HOUR 35 MINUTES · SERVES 8–10

FOR THE FILLING

2 tablespoons rapeseed oil,
    plus a little extra for greasing

3 red peppers, cored, deseeded
    and sliced

2 red onions, sliced

4 egg yolks, plus 2 whole eggs

250ml (9fl oz) double cream

½ teaspoon ground white pepper

½ teaspoon fine sea salt

125g (4½oz) mature Cheddar
    cheese, grated

1½ teaspoons chopped fresh
    chives, chopped

FOR THE PASTRY

350g (12oz) plain flour, plus a little
    extra for dusting

½ teaspoon fine sea salt

175g (6oz) unsalted butter, chilled,
    cut into cubes

2 teaspoons lemon juice

50ml (2fl oz) cold water

3 egg yolks

FOR THE TOPPING

1 × 150g (5½oz) log of goats' cheese
    with rind, sliced

½ teaspoon paprika

*Serve with buttered new potatoes
and a tomato salad with a balsamic
dressing (see page 43).*

This is a wonderful vegetarian quiche recipe that's won a hatful of Great Taste awards over the years. The chalky goats' cheese and sweet roasted peppers are a perfect match.

Place a medium frying pan on a medium heat. Add the oil along with the peppers and onions. Cook for 10–15 minutes until the peppers and onions are softened but not coloured. Transfer to a bowl to one side to cool.

To make the pastry, place the flour and salt in a large mixing bowl and stir to combine. Add the butter and rub in with your fingertips until the mixture resembles fine breadcrumbs. Make a well in the centre and add the lemon juice, then the measured water, a little bit at a time so the pastry doesn't get too wet. Use a dinner knife to incorporate the wet ingredients, then use your fingers to form the dough. If you find the pastry isn't coming together, add a further teaspoon of water. Turn the dough out on a lightly floured surface and pat into a disc. Wrap the dough in clingfilm and place in the fridge for 30 minutes.

For the filling, whisk together the egg yolks, whole egg, double cream, pepper, salt, Cheddar and chives in a large bowl or jug. Cover and place in the fridge.

Lightly butter and flour a 27cm (10¾ inch) round, loose-bottomed tart tin. When the pastry has rested, roll it out on a clean, lightly floured work surface to 3mm (⅛ inch) thick. Line the tart tin with the pastry, allowing some to hang over the side – this can be trimmed before or after baking. Cover and return to the fridge for a further 30 minutes.

Preheat the oven to 170°C fan/190°C/375°F/Gas Mark 5. Remove the pastry case from the fridge. Prick all over with a fork. Line with nonstick baking paper and fill with baking beans. Blind bake in the preheated oven for 20 minutes until cooked but not coloured. Remove the baking beans and return to the oven for a further 5–10 minutes until the base is cooked. Allow to cool a little on a wire rack.

Reduce the oven temperature to 140°C fan/160°C/325°F/Gas Mark 3.

To assemble the quiche, spoon the peppers and onions into the pastry case. Pour over the creamy filling, top with the goats' cheese slices, sprinkle over the paprika. Cook in the oven for 40–50 minutes, or until set. Allow to cool for at least 20 minutes before slicing and serving. Or chill in the fridge and serve cold.

Galettes

PREP: 15 MINUTES · COOK: 1 HOUR · SERVES 4

FOR EACH GALETTE
plain flour, for dusting
500g (1lb 2oz) block of puff pastry
1 egg yolk, beaten, or 1 tablespoon
     vegan spread, melted

No tin required – that's the only rule of galette club. These circles of puff pastry, folded in at the edges, topped with something eye-catching and mouth-watering, couldn't be easier to make – especially with shop-bought pastry. They make a perfect summer lunch. Back in the summer of 2012, we made rectangles rather than circles and sliced them into triangles so they could be arranged into a Union Jack to mark the Queen's Diamond Jubilee.

Pesto and Asparagus Galette

1 × 125g (4½oz) log of soft goats'
     cheese (no rind)
125g (4½oz) ricotta cheese
2 eggs
grated zest of 2 lemons
250g (9oz) asparagus, woody
     ends removed
olive oil, for drizzling
pastry ingredients (see above)
salt and pepper

FOR THE PESTO
100g (3½oz) basil
3 garlic cloves, roughly chopped
70g (2½oz) pine nuts (or almonds
     or walnuts), toasted
pinch of salt
olive oil, for drizzling
100g (3½oz) Parmesan cheese, grated
grated zest and juice of ½ lemon

Preheat the oven to 170°C fan/190°C/375°F/Gas Mark 5. Line a baking tray with nonstick baking paper.

To make the pesto, place most of the basil (reserving a few leaves to garnish), the garlic and the pine nuts in a food processor with a big pinch of salt. Blitz well. Drizzle in enough olive oil to loosen the mixture and blitz again. Scrape into a bowl and mix in the Parmesan and the lemon zest and juice. Season to taste.

Place the goats' cheese and ricotta in a separate bowl and mix well. Crack in the whole eggs, season and mix thoroughly again, ensuring the cheese and eggs are well combined. Add the grated zest of 1 lemon.

Place the asparagus on a plate. Drizzle with olive oil and season.

On a lightly floured surface, roll out the puff pastry to a circle measuring about 30cm (12 inches) and place on the prepared tray. Leaving a 4cm (1½ inch) border at the edge, spread the cheese mixture over the pastry to fill the circle. Swirl in a few spoonfuls of pesto. Arrange the asparagus neatly on top, then fold the border over the edges of the filling. Brush the exposed pastry with the beaten egg yolk.

Bake in the oven for 50 minutes–1 hour, or until golden and cooked through. Check and cover with tin foil if the asparagus looks a little brown. Allow to rest for 5 minutes before slicing. Sprinkle over the reserved basil and grate a little more lemon zest on top. Serve with the remaining pesto on the side for people to help themselves.

Hot-smoked Salmon and Horseradish Galette

30g (1oz) unsalted butter

2 garlic cloves, crushed

200g (7oz) spinach

300g (10½oz) soured cream

2 eggs

3 tablespoons horseradish

3 tablespoons chopped dill

200g (7oz) hot-smoked
  salmon, flaked

pastry ingredients (see page 119)

olive oil, for drizzling

pepper

Preheat the oven to 170°C fan/190°C/375°F/Gas Mark 5. Line a baking tray with nonstick baking paper.

Place a large frying pan on a medium heat. Add the butter and garlic. Stir for 1 minute, or until the garlic is cooked but not golden. Add the spinach and allow it to wilt. Remove from the heat and drain in a colander. When the spinach is cool enough to handle, spoon it into a clean tea towel and squeeze out as much moisture as you can. Chop well and place in a large mixing bowl. Stir in the soured cream and whole eggs until smooth, then add the horseradish, most of the dill and most of the salmon. Season with pepper, then fold the mixture gently with a large spoon so it's just combined.

Roll out the puff pastry as described on page 119. Leaving a 4cm (1½ inch) border at the edge, spread the creamy salmon mixture over the pastry to fill the circle. Fold the border over the edges of the filling. Brush the exposed pastry with the beaten egg yolk. Scatter the remaining salmon flakes over and drizzle with a little olive oil.

Bake in the oven for 50 minutes–1 hour, until golden and cooked through. Check and cover with aluminium foil if it's browning too much. Once cooked, sprinkle over the remaining dill. Allow to rest for 5 minutes before slicing and serving.

Tomato and Red Pepper Galette

300g (10½oz) semi-dried
    tomatoes in oil
200g (7oz) cherry tomatoes, halved
200g (7oz) roasted red peppers
    from a jar, drained and sliced
1 teaspoon dried oregano
1 tablespoon cornflour
olive oil, for drizzling
125g (4½oz) plant-based garlic
    and herb soft cheese
30g (1oz) ground almonds
pastry ingredients (see page 119)
salt and pepper
fresh oregano leaves, to garnish
    (optional)

Preheat the oven to 170°C fan/190°C/375°F/Gas Mark 5. Line a baking tray with nonstick baking paper.

Place both kinds of tomatoes in a mixing bowl with the peppers, the dried oregano and the cornflour. Season well, drizzle with a little olive oil and mix to combine. Mix the soft cheese and ground almonds in a separate bowl.

Roll out the puff pastry as described on page 119. Leaving a 4cm (1½ inch) border at the edge, spread the soft cheese mix over the pastry to fill the circle. Pile the remaining filling on top and fold the border over the edges of the filling. Brush the exposed pastry with the melted vegan spread. If using the fresh oregano leaves, toss them in a little olive oil and scatter over the galette.

Bake in the oven for 1 hour, or until golden and cooked through. Allow to rest for 5 minutes before slicing and serving.

Feta and Beetroot Galette

250g (9oz) feta cheese
200g (7oz) ricotta cheese
2 eggs
grated zest of 1 lemon
300g (10½oz) pouch of cooked
    beetroot (not in juice or vinegar)
olive oil, for drizzling
pastry ingredients (see page 119)
4 tablespoons red onion chutney
salt and pepper
a few thyme leaves, to garnish
    (optional)

Preheat the oven to 170°C fan/190°C/375°F/Gas Mark 5. Line a baking tray with nonstick baking paper.

Place 200g (7oz) of the feta in a large mixing bowl with the ricotta, eggs and lemon zest. Beat together to make a paste. Chop the beetroot into a mix of wedges and cubes. Place in a separate bowl, toss with a little olive oil and season.

Roll out the puff pastry as described on page 119. Leaving a 4cm (1½ inch) border at the edge, spread the cheese paste over the pastry to fill the circle. Dot the onion chutney on top and pile on the beetroot. Fold the border over the edges of the filling. Scatter the remaining feta over. Brush the exposed pastry with the beaten egg yolk. If using the thyme leaves, toss them in a little olive oil and scatter over the galette.

Bake in the oven for 1 hour, or until golden and cooked through. Allow to rest for 5 minutes before slicing and serving.

French Onion Tart

PREP: 40 MINUTES, PLUS CHILLING · COOK: 1 HOUR 45 MINUTES · SERVES 4

FOR THE PASTRY

300g (10½oz) plain flour, plus extra
   for dusting

pinch of salt

175g (6oz) unsalted butter, cold and
   cut into cubes

45ml (3 tablespoons) cold water

1 teaspoon lemon juice

a little oil, for greasing

1 egg yolk, beaten

FOR THE FILLING

50g (1¾oz) unsalted butter

6 onions, finely sliced

3 garlic cloves, sliced

200ml (7fl oz) vegetable stock

1 tablespoon soft brown sugar

3 tablespoons picked thyme

1 egg

30ml (2 tablespoons) double cream

70g (2½oz) Gruyère cheese, grated

salt and pepper

This can be eaten warm or cold. Cut into smaller, finger-friendly squares, it makes a great canapé for a drinks party or a pre-dinner nibble.

Low, slow cooking transforms humble onions into the star of this graceful tart – soft, sweet slivers set in a cream, cheese and thyme custard. It's so much more than the sum of its parts. And yes, using shop-bought pastry is fine if you're short on time.

First, make the pastry. Place the flour in a bowl and add a good pinch of salt. Add the butter and rub in with your fingertips until the mixture resembles rough breadcrumbs. Make a well in the centre, add the measured water and lemon juice, and mix to a rough dough. Turn the dough out on a lightly floured surface and shape into a disc. Wrap the dough in clingfilm and place in the fridge to rest.

Meanwhile, make the filling. Place a large frying pan on a medium heat. Add the butter, onions and garlic along with a pinch of salt. Reduce the heat to low and cook, stirring occasionally, for 30 minutes, or until the onions are browned and softened. Add the stock, sugar and 2 tablespoons of the thyme. Simmer for a further 10 minutes until the stock has been absorbed. Season to taste. Turn off the heat, transfer the mixture to a large bowl and leave to cool.

Preheat the oven to 170°C fan/190°C/375°F/Gas Mark 5. Lightly oil and flour a 27cm (10¾ inch) round tart tin – or you can use a square tin if you fancy a different shape. When the pastry has rested, roll it out on a clean, lightly floured work surface. This is a shallow tart, so the pastry should only be big enough to reach about halfway up the sides of the tart tin. Line the tart tin with the pastry. Prick the base of the pastry case all over with a fork. Line the case with nonstick baking paper and fill with baking beans. Blind bake in the oven for 20 minutes until cooked but not coloured. Remove the baking beans and baking paper and return the case to the oven to dry out for about 10 minutes. Remove the case from the oven, brush the beaten egg yolk over and return it to the oven for a further 5 minutes. Remove from the oven and place to one side.

Once the onion mixture has cooled, stir in the egg, double cream and 40g (1½oz) of the cheese. Spoon the filling evenly over the pastry base, allowing for a thin border around the edge. Sprinkle the remaining cheese over and cook in the oven for 30 minutes, or until the tart is golden and cooked well. Allow to sit for 5 minutes before slicing and serving.

Caramelized Shallot, Celeriac and Stilton Tarte Tatin

PREP: 15 MINUTES · COOK: 1 HOUR · SERVES 4–6

½ celeriac, about 350g (12oz), peeled and chopped into 2cm (¾ inch) cubes

2 tablespoons picked thyme, plus 8 whole sprigs

2 tablespoons rapeseed oil

50g (1¾oz) unsalted butter

10 banana shallots, halved lengthways

5 garlic cloves

2 bay leaves

2 tablespoons light soft brown sugar

2 tablespoons red wine vinegar

500g (1lb 2oz) block of puff pastry

plain flour, for dusting

1 egg yolk, beaten

150ml (5fl oz) crème fraîche

100g (3½oz) Stilton cheese, crumbled

salt and pepper

TO GARNISH

1 tablespoon chopped chives

30g (1oz) blanched hazelnuts, toasted and chopped

You can make a delicious vegan version by using vegan spread, vegan puff pastry and a mix of vegan soft cheeses with a splash of plant-based milk for the sauce.

Caramelize pretty much anything and you're on to a winner. We love the bold flavour combination of shallots, celeriac and Stilton in this pretty veggie tart, but you can swap in whatever you like: carrots, beetroot or squash; goats' cheese or feta; toasted walnuts or almonds…

Preheat the oven to 200°C fan/220°C/425°F/Gas Mark 7.

Line a medium-sized roasting tray with nonstick baking paper. Add the celeriac, picked thyme and oil. Season well, toss everything together and roast in the oven for about 25 minutes, or until it's just starting to soften.

Meanwhile, place a 24cm (9½ inch) nonstick, ovenproof frying pan on a medium heat and add the butter. When it's melted, arrange the shallots in the pan, cut-sides down, along with the garlic, bay leaves, thyme sprigs, sugar and vinegar. Reduce the heat to low and cook for 10 minutes, then remove from the heat. When the celeriac is ready, spoon it over the shallots.

Meanwhile, roll out the pastry to 5mm (¼ inch) thick and cut into a circle about 2cm (¾ inch) larger than your frying pan, then chill the pastry in the fridge on a plate lined with nonstick baking paper until the vegetables are ready.

As soon as the vegetables are cooked, remove the pastry from the fridge. Working quickly, as the pastry will start to melt, cover the shallots and celeriac with the pastry circle. Tuck the edges of the pastry into the sides of the pan so that it's snug around the edge. Cut a small hole in the centre to allow the steam to release when baking. Brush with the egg yolk and sprinkle over a little salt. Bake in the oven for 30 minutes, or until the pastry is puffed and golden.

Meanwhile, place the crème fraîche and half of the Stilton in a food processor with a big pinch of pepper. Blitz to a smooth sauce and transfer to a small bowl.

When the tart is ready, carefully ease a silicone spatula around the edges to release it from the pan, then turn it out onto a serving board or plate, so that the pastry is on the bottom. Crumble over the remaining Stilton and sprinkle over the chives and hazelnuts.

Drizzle a little of the Stilton sauce over the tart before serving in slices, or serve it alongside.

WHEN YOU HAVE MORE THAN ENOUGH, BUILD LONGER TABLES, NOT HIGHER WALLS

José Andrés

THE JOY OF COMMUNITY DINING

We've always been inspired by the roots of the word 'company'. It comes from two Latin words: *com* meaning 'with'; and *panis* meaning 'bread'. With bread. In the beginning, the company was the people with whom you shared bread. Long before it became about work, sales, tax and profit; before it became about business; the company was all about being nourished in body and soul by sharing food and human connection.

At work and in life, we could all do with tapping into the original spirit of the company. Good people. Good food. Sitting down together. Serving up joy.

We believe the world would be a better place if we ate together more. There's even some science to back us up. Professor Robin Dunbar, a top evolutionary psychologist at the University of Oxford, found that 'those who eat socially more often feel happier and are more satisfied with life, are more trusting of others, are more engaged with their local communities, and have more friends they can depend on for support.'[*]

Every day, our kitchen teams eat together for free in our canteens. Whenever we can, we get together at COOK over a meal. We've also worked with some inspiring organizations bringing people together over shared food.

The charity FoodCycle cooks meals from surplus ingredients to serve at free communal dining events for people struggling to afford a good meal. They see nourishing food and human connection as going hand-in-hand. Social isolation can be as damaging to our health as hunger.

The Long Table in Stroud, Gloucestershire, runs a warm and welcoming local restaurant with, yes, long, shared tables to eat at. They suggest a fair price for your meal and you pay what you can afford. If you can pay for somebody else's meal, you buy a token to go in the free meal pot. They wonder, 'What if everyone in our community had access to great food and someone to eat it with?' What if...? Indeed.

Wherever we have a COOK shop, we try to find a local partner organization seeking to connect people over food, and provide them with a regular, free or discounted supply of our prepared frozen meals. In every community there are people feeling isolated and lonely, for whom a shared meal will nourish both body and soul. Doing what we can to feed togetherness feels like important work. As American chef José Andrés put it, 'When you have more than enough, build longer tables, not higher walls.'

[*] 'Breaking Bread: The Functions of Social Eating', Professor Robin Dunbar, *Adaptive Human Behaviour and Physiology* 2017; 3(3): 198–211.

Get involved

We love helping bring people together over good food. If you're organizing a local event, get in touch and ask about our 30% Community Kitchen discount for groups of 20 people or more. Maybe you're part of a group that could dine together more often? Or are there people in your community you might gather to eat together? Get some inspiration from www.thelongtableonline.com and www.foodcycle.org.uk and find resources and info at www.cookfood.net/communitykitchen

'I can do things
you cannot, you can
do things I cannot,
together we can
do great things'

– Mother Teresa

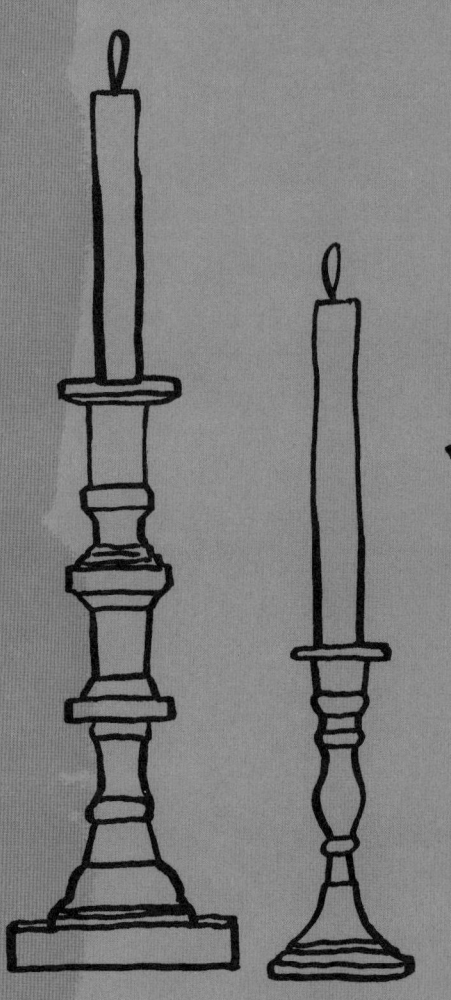

Special Nights In

Whether it's a date night or a dinner party, sometimes we want to put on a bit of a show.

These recipes will stretch and grow your kitchen confidence.

Rosemary and Sage Porchetta

PREP: 30 MINUTES, PLUS CHILLING · COOK: 2 HOURS 40 MINUTES · SERVES 4–6

FOR THE STUFFING

2 tablespoons rapeseed oil

2 tablespoons white wine vinegar

2 tablespoons Dijon mustard

1 teaspoon chilli flakes

6 garlic cloves

2 tablespoons ground fennel

finely grated zest of 3 lemons

3 tablespoons chopped sage

3 tablespoons chopped rosemary

3 tablespoons chopped flat leaf parsley

salt and pepper

FOR THE PORK

1.25–1.5kg (2lb 12oz–3lb 5oz) boneless
    pork belly, rind scored

An Italian-style hog roast made from a rolled pork belly, with a bold, herby stuffing and crisp, golden crackling. For years, we've sourced all our higher-welfare pork from the wonderfully named Dingley Dell farm in Suffolk, where they take great care of their pigs. Ask your butcher to score the rind of your pork belly and for six silicone roasting bands or some butchers' twine to hold your roll together.

Place all the stuffing ingredients into a food processor with 1 teaspoon salt and a good pinch of pepper. Blitz to a paste, then scrape into a bowl.

Place the pork belly, skin-side down, on a large chopping board. Spread the stuffing in an even layer all over the meat. Roll the pork tightly into a roulade and secure at regular intervals with six silicone roasting bands or pieces of butchers' twine.

If you want to achieve really crispy crackling, place the porchetta in a roasting tray, cover loosely with tin foil and leave in the fridge overnight, to allow the skin to dry out. When you're ready to cook the porchetta, remove it from the fridge, pat the skin dry, then season with salt just before it goes into the oven. If you're pushed for time though, season the porchetta all over with salt first, rubbing it into the skin well. Place in a roasting tray, rolled-side facing up, and loosely cover with tin foil. Place at the bottom of the fridge for 2 hours.

When you're ready to cook, preheat the oven to 170°C fan/190°C/375°F/ Gas Mark 5. Line a roasting tray in which the porchetta will fit snugly with nonstick baking paper. Remove the foil from the porchetta, transfer it to the prepared tray and roast in the oven for 2 hours. Increase the heat to 200°C fan/220°C/425°F/Gas Mark 7 for a further 30–40 minutes, or until the skin has crackled and the juices run clear.

Remove the pork from the oven and cover with tin foil. Allow to rest for 10 minutes before carving.

To carve, remove the bands or twine from the pork and use the indentations left in the meat as a guide for cutting each portion. Keep the slices thick, one per person – carving this thinly doesn't really work. Serve with roast potatoes and steamed greens. And don't forget the apple sauce – to make your own, peel, core and slice 3 apples, pop them in a saucepan with 50g (1¾oz) each of caster sugar and butter, and cook on a low heat for 15–20 minutes until the consistency of a purée.

Slow-cooked Rump of Beef in Brandy

PREP: 15 MINUTES · COOK: 4 HOURS 50 MINUTES · SERVES 4–6

1kg (2lb 4oz) rump of beef,
    cut into large pieces

2 tablespoons plain flour

3 tablespoons rapeseed oil

850ml (1½ pints) beef stock

60g (2¼oz) unsalted butter

3 onions, sliced

4 garlic cloves, sliced

400g (14oz) chestnut mushrooms,
    trimmed and sliced

1 tablespoon picked thyme

1 tablespoon chopped rosemary

2 tablespoons tomato purée

200ml (7fl oz) double cream

3 tablespoons Dijon mustard

100ml (3½fl oz) brandy

salt and pepper

3 tablespoons chopped flat leaf
    parsley, to garnish

*Serve with silky-smooth mash,
Dauphinoise Potatoes (see page 183)
or roasted new potatoes and hunks
of bread for mopping up the juices.
Add a dash of colour with your veg –
opt for Braised Red Cabbage (see
page 179), roasted carrots, sautéed
cabbage or green beans.*

Our version of the wonderfully retro Steak Diane – a popular, high-society restaurant dish of the 1940s and 1950s. Retaining a flavour 'hit' from the brandy is essential, which is why we add it near the end. The sauce is big, bold, creamy and delicious.

Place the beef in a large bowl with the flour and a good pinch each of salt and pepper. Toss together to coat well. Place a large lidded casserole dish on a medium heat. Add the oil and, in batches, brown the beef all over for 10–15 minutes. Transfer to a bowl and place to one side.

Add 100ml (3½fl oz) of the beef stock to the pan. Stir well to deglaze and release the lovely brown bits from the base of the pan. Pour the stock over the beef in the bowl and return the pan to a medium heat. Add the butter, allow it to melt, then add the onions, garlic, mushrooms, thyme and rosemary. Cook, stirring occasionally, for about 15 minutes, or until the onions and mushrooms start to soften and colour.

Preheat the oven to 160°C fan/180°C/350°F/Gas Mark 4.

Return the beef and stock to the pan, stir in the tomato purée and the remaining beef stock, and bring to a simmer. Stir well, remove from the heat and place the lid on the pan. Place in the oven and cook for about 4 hours, or until the meat is tender. Remove the lid from the pan for the last 30 minutes to help thicken the sauce.

When the beef is ready, remove the pan from the oven and stir in the cream, mustard and brandy. Return the pan to the oven for a further 20 minutes.

Remove the pan from the oven and season to taste. Sprinkle over the parsley and serve.

Pan-roasted Chicken with a Port and Red Wine Jus

PREP: 15 MINUTES · COOK: 1 HOUR 20 MINUTES · SERVES 4

FOR THE PORT AND RED WINE JUS

50g (1¾oz) unsalted butter

1 teaspoon rapeseed oil

2 shallots, finely chopped

200ml (7fl oz) port

200ml (7fl oz) red wine

1 thyme sprig

1 bay leaf

700ml (1¼ pints) beef stock

1½ tablespoons cornflour (optional)

1 tablespoon redcurrant jelly

FOR THE VEGETABLES

1 tablespoon rapeseed oil

30g (1oz) unsalted butter

8 banana shallots, halved

250g (9oz) chestnut mushrooms, trimmed and halved, larger ones quartered

3 rosemary sprigs

6 thyme sprigs

4 garlic cloves, lightly crushed but still holding their shape

FOR THE CHICKEN

4 × skin-on chicken breasts, 150–200g (5½–7oz) each

2 tablespoons rapeseed oil

1 tablespoon butter

salt and pepper

Serve with creamy mashed potato and pan-fried Savoy cabbage – shred the leaves and stir-fry with some garlic, a sprinkle of fennel or caraway seeds, and seasoning.

Elevate a standard chicken breast to a whole new level, giving it a crisp, golden skin, and serving with caramelized shallots, mushrooms and a decadent, boozy jus. A bit cheffy – and all the better for it.

First, make the jus. Place a medium saucepan on a medium heat, add 20g (¾oz) of the butter along with the oil, followed by the shallots. Stir well and cook for 10 minutes, or until golden. Add the port and wine, increase the heat to bring to the boil, then reduce to a low heat and simmer for 5 minutes, or until reduced by half. Add the thyme, bay leaf and stock and reduce by half again – this will take 10–15 minutes. If you prefer the sauce a little thicker, add the cornflour to a small bowl, spoon in a little of the sauce and stir to a paste, then whisk the paste into the sauce in the pan. Stir for 2 minutes, or until a little more thickened, then stir in the redcurrant jelly. Season to taste and remove from the heat.

Meanwhile, prepare the vegetables. Place a large frying pan on a medium heat. Add the oil and butter. When the butter has melted, place the shallots, cut-side down, in the pan and cook for 5 minutes until starting to turn golden. Turn the shallots over and add the mushrooms, herbs and garlic. Cook for 10 minutes, shaking the pan occasionally, until the mushrooms start to turn golden. Remove the pan from the heat and place to one side.

Preheat the oven to 180°C fan/200°C/400°F/Gas Mark 6. Cover the chicken breasts in the oil and season well all over. Place a large, ovenproof frying pan or casserole dish on a medium heat. Add the chicken breasts, skin-side down, and cook for 4 minutes, or until golden. Turn the chicken and cook for a further 4 minutes, then add the butter, followed by the vegetables and herbs. Place the frying pan in the oven for 20–25 minutes, or until the chicken is cooked and looking golden.

Allow the chicken to rest for 5 minutes. Strain the jus into a clean saucepan and place on a low heat. When it's warm enough, whisk in the remaining 30g (1oz) of butter, bit by bit, until you have a glossy sauce.

Slice each chicken breast into three or keep them whole. Arrange the chicken on individual plates, spoon the mushrooms and shallots on top, pour over the jus and serve.

Stuffed Chicken Cushion with Romesco Sauce

PREP: 30 MINUTES · COOK: 1 HOUR · SERVES 4

FOR THE CHICKEN

200g (7oz) cooking chorizo, peeled
    and finely chopped

100g (3½oz) mascarpone cheese
    or cream cheese

½ teaspoon white pepper

50g (1¾oz) semi-dried tomatoes
    in oil, chopped

30g (1oz) basil, most leaves chopped,
    a few leaves left whole

1 small chicken, boned (about 1kg/
    2lb 4oz without bones)

½ teaspoon sweet smoked paprika

1 tablespoon rapeseed oil

salt and pepper

FOR THE ROMESCO SAUCE

100g (3½oz) blanched almonds

150g (5½oz) roasted red peppers in oil

1 garlic clove

½ teaspoon dried oregano

2 tablespoons red wine or sherry vinegar

½ teaspoon sweet smoked paprika

3 tablespoons olive oil

salt and pepper

RECIPE CONTINUES
OVERLEAF...

A beautiful way to serve chicken in the summer, with bold, Spanish flavours and a sweet, smoky sauce. Ask your butcher to de-bone the chicken for you and for a few silicone roasting bands or some butchers' twine. Our kitchen team has mastered the tricky art of making cushions but you can try one of the easier versions in the note overleaf, if you're hesitant.

Combine the chorizo, mascarpone or cream cheese, white pepper, tomatoes and chopped basil in a large mixing bowl to make a stiff paste that can be rolled into a ball. Make sure the ball is small enough to fit inside the chicken but big enough to have the chicken wrapped snugly around it. You may have a little filling left over if you have a smaller chicken (you can add this to the roasting tray with the chicken, halfway through the cooking time).

On a large chopping board, open out the deboned chicken, skin-side down. Season well inside and out, then line with the whole basil leaves. Place the ball of filling in the centre of the chicken breasts. Cross the legs over to secure the stuffing, then turn the chicken over and tuck the skin under to keep the stuffing in and to form a round cushion – the breasts should be on top with the legs underneath. Use a silicone roasting band or piece of butchers' twine to secure the cushion around the middle, but don't pull too tightly. Wrap another band (or another piece of twine) from the top of the cushion to the bottom to make a cross and secure. Repeat twice more until you have a star shape securing the cushion well. Sprinkle the paprika over the chicken skin, pour over the oil and rub both in well to coat.

Place the cushion on a plate, cover with clingfilm and place in the fridge to chill while you make the sauce.

Place a small frying pan on a medium heat. Add the almonds and toast for 2–3 minutes until golden. Place the almonds, peppers, garlic, oregano, vinegar and paprika in a food processor with a good pinch of salt and pepper. Blitz well. Scrape down the sides of the bowl, then turn the food processor on again and pour in the oil until fully incorporated. Transfer the sauce to a serving bowl, cover with clingfilm and place in the fridge.

*Serve with Parmentier potatoes –
peel 800g–1kg (1lb 12oz–2lb 4oz)
potatoes and dice into 2cm (¾ inch)
cubes. Parboil, season well, then
toss in a tray with 2 tablespoons
preheated oil, 2 crushed garlic
cloves and the picked and finely
chopped leaves from 1 sprig of
rosemary. Roast with the chicken for
the final 30 minutes of the cooking
time at 160°C fan/180°C/350°F/
Gas Mark 4. While the chicken is
resting, turn the oven up to 180°C
fan/200°C/400°F/Gas Mark 6
and roast for a further 10 minutes.
Apart from this, a salad is all you
need, or griddled asparagus when
they are in season.*

RECIPE CONTINUED...

When you're ready to cook the chicken, preheat the oven to 160°C fan/
180°C/350°F/Gas Mark 4. Line a roasting tray with nonstick baking paper.

Place the chicken cushion on the prepared tray and cook in the oven for
35 minutes. Check the chicken and cover in tin foil if it's starting to catch.

Increase the oven temperature to 180°C fan/200°C/400°F/Gas Mark 6
and cook the chicken for a further 20 minutes. After 10 minutes, remove the
sauce from the fridge and give it a stir.

When the chicken is cooked, remove it from the oven and allow to rest for
10 minutes. It will release a lovely red oil from the chorizo. Remove the bands
or twine, carve and serve with the romesco sauce – if the sauce looks a little
split when you come to use it, just give it another good stir.

*If you've decided, not unreasonably, that the cushion is beyond you but the flavours
sound sensational (they are!), you can use skin-on chicken breasts instead – cut a
pocket in each one, spoon or pipe the stuffing inside, brown the breasts in a frying
pan, then cook in the oven for 20–25 minutes, or until golden and cooked through.
Alternatively, use a whole chicken – carefully separate the skin from the breast meat
with your fingers (taking care not to tear it), then push the stuffing into the space,
so you've effectively stuffed the breasts. Cook as for a normal roast. Don't forget to
serve the delicious romesco sauce alongside!*

Beef Wellington

PREP: 40 MINUTES, PLUS CHILLING · COOK: 1 HOUR 20 MINUTES · SERVES 6

FOR THE BEEF

1kg (2lb 4oz) beef fillet
2 tablespoons rapeseed oil
salt and pepper
Port and Red Wine Jus (see page 134), to serve

FOR THE DUXELLES

250g (9oz) mixed mushrooms (we like to use a combination of chestnut, portobello and wild)
1 tablespoon rapeseed oil
30g (1oz) unsalted butter
1 onion, finely chopped
2 garlic cloves, finely chopped
2 tablespoons picked thyme
2 tablespoons Madeira wine
1 tablespoon wholegrain mustard

FOR THE WRAPPING

4 ready-made crêpes (either shop-bought, or follow the instructions overleaf to make your own)
100g (3½oz) smooth chicken liver paté
1 teaspoon milk
1 × 500g (1lb 2oz) block of puff pastry
3 egg yolks, beaten
1 tablespoon poppy seeds

RECIPE CONTINUES OVERLEAF…

There's no getting round it: cooking a Beef Wellington from scratch is not for the faint of heart or light of wallet. When you appreciate the skill and care involved, the fact we make 500 at a time in our kitchen is quite remarkable. The glossy, sophisticated sauce is a must. The late Clarissa Dickson Wright, one half of TV's *Two Fat Ladies*, proclaimed it to be as good as any she'd ever tasted, when she visited us to do some filming.

Preheat the oven to 200°C fan/220°C/425°F/Gas Mark 7.

Place the beef in a roasting tray. Season with a generous grinding of pepper, drizzle over the oil and rub in well. Place the tray in the oven for 15 minutes to seal the meat. Remove the tray from the oven and transfer the meat to a board. Roll the meat in clingfilm to make a sausage, wrap up each end well and place in the fridge to chill. Turn off the oven for now.

Meanwhile, make the duxelles. Place the mushrooms in a food processor and blitz to the texture of rough breadcrumbs. Alternatively, you can chop the mushrooms very finely by hand. Place a medium frying pan on a medium heat and add the oil and butter. When the butter has melted, add the onion, garlic and thyme to the pan. Cook for about 10 minutes, stirring continuously, until the onions are softened. Add the mushrooms and the Madeira wine, then fry for 15–20 minutes, stirring well, until all the liquid is released and the mushrooms are starting to dry out. Season well and stir in the mustard, then remove from the heat and place to one side.

Lay two large pieces of clingfilm out on a clean work surface. Lay the 4 crêpes on the clingfilm in two rows, slightly overlapping (you can trim them to size if you need to). Place the chicken liver paté in a bowl and mix with the milk until smooth and spreadable. Dot small spoonfuls of the paté evenly over the crêpes. Spoon the duxelles over the crêpes and spread out in an even layer. Unwrap the fillet of beef and place along the centre of the crêpes. Using the clingfilm, roll the crêpes over the beef, then twist the clingfilm to make a tight sausage. Place on a tray and put in the fridge to chill while you roll out the pastry.

Amp up the indulgence and serve with Dauphinoise Potatoes (see page 183). For veg, go with Creamed Spinach (see page 179), French beans sautéed with garlic or Braised Red Cabbage (see page 179). Whole heritage carrots, glazed in honey and roasted, are another great option.

RECIPE CONTINUED...

Line a large oven tray with nonstick baking paper. On a lightly floured work surface, roll out one-third of the puff pastry to about 20 × 30cm (8 × 12 inches) – it should be big enough for a 3cm (1¼ inch) border once the beef is placed on top. Roll out the remaining pastry to about 30 × 35cm (12 × 14 inches) – it should be big enough to cover the beef completely and have a border to match up with the other piece of pastry. Place the smaller piece of pastry onto the prepared tray. Unwrap the beef from the clingfilm and place on the pastry, with a border all around. Brush the border and the crêpe-covered beef with some of the beaten egg yolks. Carefully drape the larger piece of pastry over the beef so that the two borders line up. Gently press the pastry down around the beef to seal it in well. Make sure a neat border remains and trim any excess. Use a fork to press into the pastry to crimp the edges. Brush the pastry all over with a thin layer of the beaten egg yolks. Place the Beef Wellington in the fridge to chill for at least 30 minutes.

When you're ready to cook, preheat the oven to 180°C fan/200°C/400°F/Gas Mark 6. Take the beef out of the fridge and allow it to rest at room temperature for 10–15 minutes before cooking. Glaze it with more of the beaten egg yolks and sprinkle over the poppy seeds. Bake in the oven for about 30 minutes for medium-rare or 35 minutes for medium, allowing the pastry to become golden and crisp. Remove from the oven and allow to rest for 5–10 minutes before carving.

Meanwhile, prepare the Port and Red Wine Jus as described on page 134. Once the butter has melted and is combined with the jus, serve it alongside the Beef Wellington.

To make your own crêpes, sift 100g (3½oz) plain flour into a large mixing bowl, make a well in the centre and crack in 2 eggs. Whisk the eggs into the flour, adding 100ml (3½fl oz) milk, little by little, when the mixture begins to thicken. Whisk until you have smooth batter. Add a pinch of sea salt and 1 tablespoon of finely chopped herbs (chives, thyme or parsley, or a mixture) and whisk again. Heat 1 tablespoon of oil in a frying pan over a high heat. Add some batter, quickly swirl it around the pan and pour out the excess to give a really thin pancake. Once cooked lightly on one side, turn and cook on the other side (you don't want the crêpes to have too much colour). Repeat until you have enough crêpes to cover the beef.

Huntsman's Chicken

PREP: 25 MINUTES · COOK: 1 HOUR 50 MINUTES · SERVES 4

FOR THE DUXELLES

250g (9oz) chestnut mushrooms,
    trimmed

20g (¾oz) unsalted butter

1 teaspoon olive oil

2 shallots, finely chopped

2 garlic cloves, finely chopped

6 thyme sprigs, leaves picked
    and chopped

2 tablespoons marsala wine

100ml (3½fl oz) mushroom or chicken
    stock or water

20g (¾oz) Grana Padano or Parmesan
    cheese, grated

2 tablespoons double cream (optional)

FOR THE SAUCE

300ml (10fl oz) Merlot wine

100ml (3½fl oz) marsala wine

3 bay leaves

400ml (14fl oz) chicken stock

200ml (7fl oz) mushroom stock

2 tablespoons redcurrant jelly

2 tablespoons cornflour

FOR THE CHICKEN

4 chicken breasts, each about
    150g (5½oz)

4 bay leaves

4–8 sweet-cure streaky bacon rashers,
    depending on their size

1 tablespoon olive oil

salt and pepper

*Dauphinoise Potatoes (see page 183)
or creamy mash are the perfect match,
with Braised Red Cabbage (page 179)
and roasted carrots.*

Slicing into a chicken breast to find a hidden pocket of intensely flavoured mushroom duxelles is what gives this dish its wow factor. The marsala and red wine sauce brings everything together in spectacular fashion. There's a fair bit of kitchen skill involved but it's worth it – once you get the hang of the technique, you can invent your own stuffing flavours (goats' cheese and sun-dried tomatoes is great in the summer).

First, make the duxelles. Place the mushrooms in a food processor and blitz until finely chopped. Alternatively, chop the mushrooms very finely by hand. Place a large nonstick frying pan on a medium heat, then add the butter and oil. When the butter has melted, add the mushrooms, shallots, garlic and thyme. Cook for 20 minutes, stirring occasionally, until the liquid is released and the mixture is starting to dry out. Increase the heat to high, then add the marsala and stock or water. Allow to bubble and soften for 5–10 minutes until the liquid has evaporated. Season to taste, then remove from the heat, transfer to a bowl and stir in the cheese and cream (if using). Allow to cool at room temperature.

Now make the sauce. Place all the ingredients except the cornflour in a medium saucepan. Bring to the boil, then reduce to a simmer for about 45 minutes until the sauce has reduced and is thick enough to coat the back of a spoon.

Once the duxelles has cooled, prepare the chicken. Place the chicken breasts face down on a chopping board and cut a long pocket into the back of each breast – you want to cut through to the centre, but not out the other side. Spoon the duxelles into a piping bag and pipe the stuffing into each breast. Place a bay leaf on top and wrap each breast with one or two rashers of bacon. Secure with cocktail sticks, if needed. Place the chicken breasts on a plate and cover with clingfilm. Chill in the fridge until needed.

When you're ready to cook the chicken, preheat the oven to 180°C fan/200°C/400°F/Gas Mark 6. Place a large nonstick frying pan on a medium heat and add the oil. Brown the chicken breasts all over for about 10 minutes (you may need to do this in batches), then transfer to a medium roasting tray and place in the oven for 20–25 minutes until golden and cooked through.

Warm the sauce up again. Add the cornflour to a small bowl, spoon in a little of the sauce and stir to a paste, then whisk the paste into the sauce in the pan. Stir for 2 minutes, or until a little thicker, then season to taste and remove from the heat. Divide the chicken between individual plates, spoon over the sauce and serve.

Slow-roasted Spiced Shoulder of Lamb with Mango Chutney

PREP: 25 MINUTES, PLUS MARINATING · COOK: 4–5 HOURS · SERVES 6–8

1.7kg (3lb 12oz) bone-in shoulder of lamb

50g (1¾oz) fresh coriander, chopped, to garnish

FOR THE MARINADE

1 tablespoon fennel seeds

4 green cardamom pods, crushed and seeds removed

few curry leaf sprigs, leaves picked, or ½ tablespoon dried curry leaves (optional)

2 tablespoons ground cumin

1 tablespoon ground coriander

1 tablespoon Madras curry powder

1 teaspoon chilli powder

1 thumb-sized piece of fresh ginger, grated

4 garlic cloves, crushed

250ml (9fl oz) natural yoghurt

grated zest and juice of 2 limes

salt and pepper

FOR THE MANGO CHUTNEY

1 tablespoon cumin seeds

1 tablespoon coriander seeds

1 cinnamon stick

½ teaspoon chilli flakes

1 teaspoon nigella seeds

1 teaspoon rapeseed oil

2 shallots, finely chopped

2 garlic cloves, finely sliced

pinch of salt

500g (1lb 2oz) fresh mango, diced

1 teaspoon ground turmeric

200ml (7fl oz) white wine vinegar

50g (1¾oz) soft brown sugar

A 'wow' way to serve roast lamb, especially in the summer. Making your own mango chutney might sound like overkill but it's worth the effort – the flavour match is made in heaven. Don't worry if the yoghurt marinade looks split once cooked – just stir it up and mix with the shredded lamb.

Start with the marinade. Place the fennel seeds, cardamom seeds and curry leaves (if using) in a pestle and mortar with a good pinch of salt. Grind well, then tip into a roasting tray or an extra-large freezer bag. Add the remaining marinade ingredients with a teaspoon each of salt and pepper. Poke the lamb all over with a metal skewer. Add the lamb to the roasting tray or freezer bag and massage the marinade into the meat. Cover the tray or seal the bag and place in the fridge overnight to marinate.

One hour before you're ready to cook, remove the lamb from the fridge and allow to come up to room temperature. Preheat the oven to 150°C fan/170°C/335°F/Gas Mark 3½.

Uncover the lamb and place it in a large roasting tray if it's not already in one. Pour over the marinade, cover tightly in tin foil and place in the oven to slow cook for 4–5 hours, or until the meat is tender and cooked through.

Meanwhile, make the mango chutney. Place a medium saucepan on a low heat and add the cumin seeds, coriander seeds, cinnamon stick, chilli flakes and nigella seeds. Toast for 1 minute, or until smelling delicious, then transfer to a bowl. Return the saucepan to the heat and add the oil, followed by the shallots and garlic with a pinch of salt. Cook for about 5 minutes, or until the shallots are turning transparent. Add the remaining ingredients, including the toasted whole spices, turn up the heat and bring to the boil, then reduce the heat to a simmer. Cook on low for 5–10 minutes, stirring occasionally, until the sugar has dissolved and the mango is cooked but holding its shape. Remove from the heat, transfer to a bowl and allow to cool.

When the lamb is ready, shred or slice the meat and spoon over any cooking juices. Scatter the coriander on top and serve with the mango chutney.

Serve with warm naan, a couscous salad (see the serving suggestion on page 25) and some caramelized lime halves for squeezing over.

Salmon Wellington

PREP: 35 MINUTES · COOK: 1 HOUR 5 MINUTES · SERVES 4

1 raw beetroot, scrubbed, peeled
    and roughly chopped

2 tablespoons white wine vinegar

10g (¼oz) dill, chopped

50g (1¾oz) mascarpone cheese

1 tablespoon horseradish

2 × 320g (11¼oz) ready-rolled
    all butter puff pastry sheets

600g (1lb 5oz) piece of salmon fillet,
    skinless and boneless

1 egg yolk, beaten

*Serve with minted new potatoes or
Dauphinoise Potatoes (see page 183).
Roast fennel (sliced, drizzled with
oil, seasoned and roasted) is a lovely
flavour match. Or go with seasonal
greens, such as broccoli, wilted
spinach, Creamed Spinach (see
page 179) or green beans. Dill sauce
is great on the side, or make a simple
horseradish cream by mixing a few
spoonfuls of horseradish with a little
crème fraîche.*

Salmon and beetroot is a match made in heaven, if only for the glorious, sunset colours. This looks and sounds like a tricky recipe but is surprisingly straightforward. You can use individual salmon portions instead of a whole fillet – leave a small gap between each one so the pastry makes natural indentations when it cooks, then you can use these as a guide for cutting each portion.

Place the beetroot into a food processor and pulse until finely chopped. Alternatively, you can chop by hand, but make sure it's really finely chopped (you might want to wear gloves as it can get quite messy). Tip the beetroot into a saucepan, add the vinegar, along with 50ml (2fl oz) water, and mix. Place on a low heat and cook for about 30 minutes, stirring occasionally, until the water has evaporated and the beetroot is just cooked. Transfer to a bowl, season and put to one side to cool.

Place the dill, mascarpone and horseradish in a bowl and mix to a smooth, thick paste.

Preheat the oven to 180°C fan/200°C/400°F/Gas Mark 6. Line a baking tray with nonstick baking paper.

Unroll the pastry sheets. Place one sheet on the prepared tray and place the salmon in the middle. Spoon the beetroot over the salmon and dot the dill cream on top. Brush the pastry around the salmon with some of the beaten egg yolks. Drape the second sheet of pastry over the salmon and gently use the side of your hands to bind the edges of the pastry and ensure the salmon is secured tightly in the pastry parcel. Trim the pastry, if needed, but allow a 4cm (1½ inch) border all the way around. Use a fork to press into the pastry to crimp the edges. Brush the pastry all over with more beaten egg yolks and prick a hole in the top to allow the steam to escape.

Place the Salmon Wellington in the oven for 25–35 minutes until the pastry is golden and the salmon is just cooked through. Allow to sit for 5 minutes before slicing and serving.

Crab and Fennel Tortiglioni

PREP: 15 MINUTES · COOK: 25 MINUTES · SERVES 4

2 tablespoons olive oil

1 fennel bulb, finely chopped

4 shallots, finely chopped

1 teaspoon fennel seeds, crushed

20g (¾oz) flat leaf parsley, leaves picked and chopped, stalks finely chopped

2 anchovy fillets, in oil

150ml (5fl oz) dry white wine

100g (3½oz) fresh picked brown crab meat

200ml (7fl oz) fish stock

325g (11½oz) dried tortiglioni pasta

100g (3½oz) fresh picked white crab meat

100ml (3½fl oz) double cream

2 tablespoons lemon juice

salt and pepper

TO GARNISH

1 red chilli, finely chopped

grated zest of 1 lemon

Crab always feels like a bit of a luxury and this dish is a real treat for seafood lovers. The subtle aniseed of the fennel married with cream, wine and then the holy trinity of lemon, chilli and parsley, leaves this teetering on heavenly. In our kitchen, we make this with linguine but tortiglioni is the ideal pasta: big, barrel-like tubes with ridges that hold a sauce really well. Rigatoni will also do, or even penne, and linguine is fine, too. So, basically, whatever pasta you like!

Place a large frying pan on a medium heat. Add the olive oil followed by the fennel, shallots, fennel seeds and parsley stalks. Cook for 10 minutes, stirring continuously, until the fennel has softened. Add the anchovy fillets and break them down with a wooden spoon. Increase the heat and stir in the white wine. Reduce to a simmer and allow the wine to reduce by half – this will take 2–3 minutes.

Add the brown crab meat and fish stock, stir and allow to simmer on a low heat for a few minutes while you cook the pasta.

Cook the pasta in a large pan of salted water according to the packet instructions until al dente. Drain, saving a cup of the pasta water to add later.

Tip the pasta into the frying pan. Add the white crab meat, then stir in the cream along with a splash of the reserved pasta water. Allow to simmer for 1 minute, tossing the pasta into the sauce. Add the lemon juice and season to taste.

Divide the pasta between individual serving bowls, scatter over the chilli, lemon zest and chopped parsley leaves, and serve.

Extra wedges of lemon make a lovely garnish, and a side salad of pea shoots, sun-dried tomatoes, chopped parsley and some dill sprigs is perfect.

Stuffed Sea Bass with Fennel and Dill

PREP: 25 MINUTES · COOK: 50 MINUTES · SERVES 4

2 large fennel bulbs, sliced
(reserving any leafy fronds)

4 tablespoons rapeseed oil

3 lemons

30g (1oz) flat leaf parsley, chopped

15g (½oz) fresh coriander, chopped

15g (½oz) mint, leaves picked
and chopped

30g (1oz) dill, chopped

2 tablespoons baby capers,
drained and chopped

1 teaspoon caster sugar

4 butterflied sea bass, 300–400g
(10½–14oz) each, skin on

salt and pepper

sherry vinegar, to serve

This dish just begs to be eaten in the garden, on a warm summer's evening, with a glass of something crisp and chilled. Ask your fishmonger to butterfly the sea bass for you, or use eight fillets with the skin on. You'll need silicone roasting bands or butchers' twine to secure the stuffed fish.

Preheat the oven to 180°C fan/200°C/400°F/Gas Mark 6. Place the fennel in a roasting tray with 2 tablespoons of the oil and season. Grate over the zest of one lemon and toss to coat. Place the tray in the oven for 25 minutes, turning three times during the cooking, until softened and turning golden. Remove the tray from the oven and allow the fennel to cool.

Put the zest of one lemon into the bowl of a food processor. Add all the herbs and pulse to chop. Scrape down the sides of the bowl, then add the cooled fennel along with the capers and sugar. Season. Pulse again until the fennel is roughly chopped and well combined. Transfer the stuffing mixture to a bowl and place to one side.

When you're ready to cook, line two roasting trays with nonstick baking paper. Place two sea bass on each tray, season them well inside and out and drizzle the remaining oil over. Take the stuffing mixture and spoon evenly into each fish, then close and press gently to secure. Slice the remaining lemon into slices and place one slice on top of each fish. Use three silicone roasting bands or pieces of butchers' twine at even intervals to secure each bass and keep the stuffing in. Cook in the oven for 20–25 minutes, or until the fish is tender.

Remove from the oven and allow the fish to rest for 2 minutes before serving. Carefully remove the bands or twine. Scatter over any fennel fronds and add a sprinkling of sherry vinegar before serving.

Serve with buttered or roasted new potatoes and a crisp green salad, perhaps with a simple anchovy dressing – mash up 2 anchovy fillets and shake in a jam jar with 6 tablespoons olive oil, 2 tablespoons red wine vinegar and some seasoning. Charred little gem lettuce is another good option – remove the loose, outer leaves, then quarter, rub with olive oil and grill or toast in a pan until lightly charred.

Nut Roast with Balsamic Red Onions

PREP: 30 MINUTES · COOK: 1 HOUR 30 MINUTES · SERVES 4–6

FOR THE ONION TOPPING
2 red onions, sliced

2 tablespoons balsamic vinegar

2 tablespoons caster sugar

100ml (3½fl oz) vegetable stock

FOR THE NUT ROAST
100g (3½ oz) dried apricots, chopped

50ml (2fl oz) Madeira wine

300g (10½oz) mixed unsalted nuts
(we use a combination of cashews,
brazils and almonds)

1 vegetable stock cube

1 tablespoon olive oil, plus extra
for greasing

30g (1oz) unsalted butter

2 onions, finely chopped

2 garlic cloves, chopped

1 tablespoon dried sage

200g (7oz) chestnut mushrooms,
trimmed and chopped

3 tablespoons desiccated coconut

100g (3½oz) fresh breadcrumbs

10g (¼oz) flat leaf parsley, chopped

2 eggs

salt and pepper

fresh thyme sprigs, to garnish
(optional)

An unapologetically old-school nut roast recipe that we've been making for 20 years. Every time we try to improve it, we end up coming back to the original. The sweetness of the Madeira-soaked apricots and balsamic red onions perfectly balances out the medley of nuts and meaty mushrooms.

To make the topping, place the red onions in a saucepan with the vinegar, sugar and stock. Bring to the boil, then reduce to a simmer. Cook for about 15 minutes, or until softened, then remove from the heat and place to one side.

Place the apricots in a bowl with the Madeira wine and leave to soak.

Meanwhile, place the nuts and the stock cube in a food processor and blitz until finely chopped.

Place a large nonstick frying pan on a medium heat, then add the oil and butter. When the butter has melted, add the onions, garlic and sage. Allow to cook on a low heat for about 10 minutes until the onions are translucent and softened. Add the mushrooms and stir. Cook for a further 10 minutes. Remove from the heat and transfer the mixture to a large mixing bowl. Stir in the chopped apricots along with the Madeira wine, the chopped nuts and the coconut, breadcrumbs, parsley and eggs. Season and mix well.

Preheat the oven to 180°C fan/200°C/400°F/Gas Mark 6. Grease and line a 900g (2lb) loaf tin with nonstick baking paper.

Spoon the onion topping mixture into the base of the prepared tin and pat down. Spoon the nut mixture into the tin and pat down. Grease a piece of tin foil and place over the top. Bake in the centre of the oven for 30 minutes, then remove the foil and bake for a further 20 minutes until golden and cooked through.

When you're ready to serve, turn the nut roast out onto a serving board, remove the baking paper, garnish with fresh thyme sprigs (if using) and slice.

Serve with all your usual favourite trimmings for a roast. You can use the same mix as a topping for big field mushrooms – just spoon it into the well of each mushroom, grate over a vegetarian hard cheese and bake in the oven. This mix also makes a great stuffing for a joint of meat.

Portobello Mushroom Risotto

PREP: 15 MINUTES · COOK: 45 MINUTES · SERVES 4 AS A MAIN COURSE OR 8 AS A STARTER

450g (1lb) mix of portobello and chestnut mushrooms, trimmed

1.2 litres (2 pints) mushroom stock

40g (1½oz) dried porcini mushrooms

2 tablespoons olive oil

70g (2½oz) unsalted butter

1 onion, finely chopped

2 garlic cloves, finely chopped

1 tablespoon picked thyme

300g (10½oz) risotto rice

200ml (7fl oz) white wine

50ml (2fl oz) marsala wine (optional)

150ml (5fl oz) double cream

50g (1¾oz) Parmesan cheese, grated, plus extra to serve

salt and pepper

2 tablespoons chopped flat leaf parsley, to serve

Smaller portions make a good starter for a dinner party. Add a drizzle of truffle oil to make it extra special. Serve with a rocket and Parmesan salad on the side, with a balsamic dressing (see page 43).

When we cracked the code of how to freeze a risotto there was widespread rejoicing (sorry, we're sworn to secrecy on that one). So, here we have a traditionally made version of our award-winning mushroom recipe – rich, earthy, creamy… It's simultaneously classy and comforting.

Slice one of the portobello mushrooms and put it to one side to cook later for a garnish. Finely chop the rest of the mushrooms.

Place the mushroom stock in a saucepan and bring to the boil. Reduce to a simmer and add the dried mushrooms. Stir well and leave the pan on a low heat to keep warm.

Place a large, shallow cast-iron pan or frying pan on a medium heat. Add the olive oil and half of the butter. When the butter has melted, add the onion, garlic and thyme. Cook for about 5 minutes, stirring, until the onion has softened and looks translucent. Mix in the chopped mushrooms and stir for a further 5–10 minutes. Add the rice and keep stirring for a further 2 minutes. Increase the heat and add the white wine and the marsala (if using). Stir well, then reduce the heat and allow the liquid to reduce by half – this will take 2–3 minutes.

Strain the stock through a sieve into a clean saucepan and place back on the heat. Chop the rehydrated mushrooms and add to the risotto pan. Add the warm stock to the risotto pan, one ladle at a time, stirring continuously. Wait until each ladle of stock has been absorbed before you add another. This will take about 20 minutes. The rice will be cooked with a little bite. Turn off the heat, season, pour in the cream and add the cheese. Stir, then place a lid on the saucepan and allow the risotto to sit for 5 minutes.

Meanwhile, place a small frying pan on a medium heat. Add the remaining butter followed by the reserved sliced portobello mushroom. Fry for 5 minutes until crisp and cooked. Season with a little salt.

Stir the risotto, then divide between individual serving dishes. Serve topped with the sliced mushrooms along with a sprinkling of parsley and extra Parmesan.

Lamb Shanks with a Redcurrant and Rosemary Jus

PREP: 10 MINUTES · COOK: 3 HOURS · SERVES 4

4 lamb shanks, about 450g (1lb) each

5 tablespoons rapeseed oil

1 onion, finely chopped

4 garlic cloves, chopped

2 celery sticks, chopped

2 carrots, chopped

3 tablespoons plain flour

300ml (10fl oz) red wine

1 tablespoon redcurrant jelly

600ml (20fl oz) lamb stock

1 tablespoon tomato purée

3 rosemary sprigs

1 tablespoon cornflour (optional)

salt and pepper

A gastropub classic that's surprisingly straightforward to make, as long as you have time for the slow cooking. Pop it in the oven on a gloomy autumn afternoon, nip out for a walk and return to a kitchen smelling of heavenly promise. It's a lovely dish to have in the freezer so, if you can add a couple of extra shanks to your pot, definitely do so.

Preheat the oven to 140°C fan/160°C/325°F/Gas Mark 3.

Season the lamb shanks. Place a large, lidded casserole pan on a medium heat. Add 1½ tablespoons of the oil and brown the lamb shanks in two batches, turning them so that they are golden brown all over – this will take about 10 minutes. Transfer to a plate and place to one side.

Return the pan to the heat with the remaining oil. Add the onion, garlic, celery and carrots. Fry for about 10 minutes, stirring occasionally, until just starting to colour. Add the flour and stir to coat the vegetables. Pour in the wine and allow to simmer for a couple of minutes, then add the remaining ingredients, except the cornflour, and season with salt and pepper. Return the shanks to the pan and nestle them in so the bones are pointing upwards. Cover the pan with a piece of tin foil and place the lid on top. Place the pan in the oven for 2½ hours, or until the lamb is tender but not falling off the bone.

If you would like a slightly thicker sauce, carefully remove the shanks to another ovenproof dish, cover with tin foil and place in the oven on a low heat to keep warm. Strain the liquid from the casserole pan into a frying pan, keeping the cooking vegetables in the sieve. Place the frying pan on a medium heat and allow the liquid to reduce a little. Skim the fat from the top, if you like. Stir in the cornflour. Once the sauce is at the desired consistency, return the vegetables to the sauce and season to taste. Place the lamb shanks in individual serving dishes and spoon the sauce over, along with the vegetables.

Serve with buttery mashed potato or Dauphinoise Potatoes (see page 183), and Creamed Spinach (see page 179), Braised Red Cabbage (see page 179) or sautéed cabbage.

Venison Casserole

PREP: 15 MINUTES · COOK: 2 HOURS 10 MINUTES–2 HOURS 40 MINUTES · SERVES 4–6

800g–1kg (1lb 12oz–2lb 4oz) venison
    haunch or shoulder, diced

about 4 tablespoons plain flour

3 tablespoons olive oil

200ml (7fl oz) Merlot wine

30g (1oz) unsalted butter

2 onions, chopped

4 garlic cloves, chopped

4 rosemary sprigs

6 thyme sprigs

4 bay leaves

300g (10½oz) chestnut mushrooms,
    trimmed and sliced

6 dried juniper berries

½ teaspoon ground cinnamon

½ teaspoon ground ginger

¼ teaspoon ground cloves

2 tablespoons tomato purée

400ml (14fl oz) beef stock

2 tablespoons redcurrant jelly
    or cranberry sauce

30g (1oz) dried cranberries

150g (5½oz) vacuum-packed
    dried chestnuts

salt and pepper

This dish appears on our menu every autumn to take us through the winter. It's perfect for the festive season, with sweet chestnuts, cranberries and spices added to the rich, red wine sauce. For years, we've bought our venison from Ben Rigby, who sources game from the UK's finest country estates.

Place the diced venison in a large mixing bowl and sprinkle over enough flour to coat the meat pieces. Season and toss to coat. Place a large, lidded casserole dish on a medium heat. Add 1 tablespoon of the oil and, in batches, add the venison pieces to the pan to brown all over. Once browned, transfer each batch to a bowl to one side. Add more oil to the pan, if needed, and repeat with the remaining meat. When all the venison is browned, add a splash of the wine to the hot pan and scrape the sides with a wooden spoon to deglaze the pan. Pour this liquid over the venison and wipe out the pan with a piece of kitchen paper.

Preheat the oven to 160°C fan/180°C/350°F/Gas Mark 4.

Place the casserole dish back on a medium heat and add the butter. When the butter has melted, add the onions and garlic. Reduce the heat and cook for about 5 minutes until the onions are starting to soften. Add the fresh herbs and mushrooms and cook for a further 10 minutes. Add the dried spices and tomato purée. Cook, stirring, for 2 minutes. Return the venison to the pan and add the rest of the wine and the remaining ingredients. Season and give everything a good stir. Bring to a simmer, then turn off the heat.

Place the lid on the casserole and place in the oven for 1½–2 hours, or until the venison is tender and the sauce slightly thickened. When the casserole is ready, remove the whole herbs, season to taste and serve.

Don't hold back – serve this with Dauphinoise Potatoes (see page 183), Braised Red Cabbage (see page 179), steamed Tenderstem broccoli or sautéed Brussels sprouts – cut your sprouts in half, heat 1 tablespoon oil in a pan on a medium–high heat and sauté the sprouts until the edges turn golden, then add a generous knob of butter and some crushed garlic for the last few minutes, season and serve.

'No act of kindness,
no matter how small,
is ever wasted'

– Aesop

KITCHEN WISDOM NO.5

Salads and Sides

Often, it's the supporting act that
makes the star shine most brightly.

These are our go-to accompaniments
to enhance your main course.

Griddled Vegetable Minted Couscous

PREP: 25 MINUTES · COOK: 30 MINUTES · SERVES 6–8

1 red onion, cut into 6 wedges

1 green pepper, cored, deseeded
    and thinly sliced

100g (3½oz) chestnut mushrooms,
    trimmed and halved

1 courgette, sliced

2 tablespoons olive oil

150g (5½oz) couscous

250ml (9fl oz) vegetable stock

70g (2½oz) sun-dried tomatoes
    in oil, chopped, plus 4 tablespoons
    of the oil

1 tablespoon runny honey

10g (¼oz) mint, leaves picked
    and chopped

grated zest of 1 lemon, plus
    2 tablespoons lemon juice

40g (1½oz) flaked almonds, toasted

40g (1½oz) shelled pistachios,
    toasted and chopped

salt and pepper

Bring couscous to life with a vibrant, mint dressing, some lightly charred vegetables and sun-dried tomatoes. If you're in a rush and don't have time to griddle the veg, use diced fresh peppers and cucumber instead – with the sun-dried tomatoes and the dressing, it will still be delicious. This can be served either warm or cold.

Place a griddle pan on a medium heat. Put the vegetables in a large mixing bowl, add the olive oil and mix well. Season well. In batches, griddle the vegetables until charred and a little softened. This will take about 30 minutes. Roughly chop the griddled vegetables or leave them whole, transfer to a large salad bowl and put to one side to cool a little.

Meanwhile, cook the couscous according to the packet instructions using the vegetable stock. Once cooked, fluff up and allow to cool a little.

Add the couscous to the salad bowl along with the sun-dried tomatoes. In a small bowl, whisk together the oil from the sun-dried tomatoes, the honey, most of the mint leaves, the lemon zest and lemon juice. Season to taste and pour over the vegetables and couscous. Add most of the nuts and toss everything together.

Spoon the salad onto a platter or into a serving bowl and scatter over the remaining mint and nuts.

This is fantastic with chicken or lamb dishes in the summer. Try it with Moroccan-spiced Harissa Chicken (see page 25), Piri-piri Drumsticks Traybake (see page 55), or Roasted Red Pepper and Goats' Cheese Quiche (see page 116).

Wild Rice Salad with Ginger and Lime Dressing

PREP: 15 MINUTES · COOK: 20–45 MINUTES · SERVES 6–8

150g (5½oz) wild rice or wild rice mix
(ready-cooked rice mixes make this
very quick and easy)
100g (3½oz) radishes, sliced
100g (3½oz) feta cheese, crumbled
¼ small watermelon or cantaloupe
melon, total weight 300g (10½oz),
cut into small chunks
30g (1oz) dried cranberries
juice of 1 lime
4cm (1½ inch) piece of fresh root ginger,
peeled and grated
½ garlic clove, crushed
1 teaspoon honey
4 tablespoons rapeseed oil
70g (2½oz) mixed nuts and
seeds, toasted
100g (3½oz) mixed salad leaves
salt and pepper

A salad you could happily eat on its own, with its kaleidoscope of flavours and textures. The wild rice (not actually a rice, but a grain!) has a lovely nutty taste and firm texture that contrasts with the soft, sweet melon. Add in crunchy radishes and creamy feta, and give it all a boost with a bold and zesty dressing, and you have a salad that doesn't hold back. The dressing is fabulous on any salad.

Cook the rice according to the packet instructions. Drain in a sieve and cool under cold running water. Tip the rice into a large mixing bowl. Add the radishes, feta, watermelon or melon and cranberries.

In a small bowl, whisk together the lime juice, ginger, garlic, honey and oil. Season to taste and whisk again. Pour the dressing over the wild rice salad.

Add the nuts, seeds and mixed salad leaves, then toss again. Transfer to a serving bowl or platter.

This is great as part of a summer barbecue or with a slow roast. Try it with Sticky Barbecue Ribs (see page 52), Slow-roasted Spiced Shoulder of Lamb with Mango Chutney (see page 145) or French Onion Tart (see page 123).

Lebanese-style Salad

PREP: 20 MINUTES · COOK: 25 MINUTES · SERVES 6–8

2 pitta breads, wholemeal or white, cut into bite-sized pieces

5 tablespoons rapeseed oil

2 tablespoons za'atar

1 cucumber, halved lengthways and seeds scooped out

4 vine-ripened tomatoes, chopped

½ small red or white cabbage, finely sliced (with a mandoline or knife)

20g (¾oz) dill, chopped

20g (¾oz) flat leaf parsley, chopped

20g (¾oz) mint, leaves picked and chopped

2 tablespoons pomegranate molasses

2 tablespoons red wine vinegar

100g (3½oz) feta cheese, crumbled

50g (1¾oz) pomegranate seeds

salt and pepper

This Lebanese-style chopped salad, known as *fattoush*, is eaten everywhere (and with everything) in the Middle East. Its hallmarks are a refreshing crispness, fried or toasted bread, and liberal use of fresh herbs – after that, just about anything goes. Our version includes feta and a lovely, sweet pomegranate dressing. A bowl of this alongside any summer meal will bring smiles to the table.

Preheat the oven to 200°C fan/220°C/425°F/Gas Mark 7.

Place the pitta bread pieces in a large roasting tray and toss with 2 tablespoons of the oil, the za'tar and a pinch of salt. Bake in the oven for 20–25 minutes, tossing halfway through the cooking time, until golden and crunchy. Remove from the oven and place to one side.

Slice the cucumber into half moons and place in a large salad bowl. Add the tomatoes, cabbage and all the chopped herbs.

In a separate bowl, whisk the remaining oil with the pomegranate molasses and vinegar. Season well.

Just before serving, pour the dressing over the salad and add the feta, the pomegranate seeds and crispy pitta bread pieces to the bowl. Toss well to coat, then transfer to a serving bowl or platter and serve.

Serve this with chicken, fish or lamb for a tasty summer side. Try it with Stuffed Sea Bass with Fennel and Dill (see page 153), Moroccan-spiced Harissa Chicken (see page 25) or Vegetable Moussaka (see page 76).

Coleslaw with Toasted Halloumi

PREP: 20 MINUTES · COOK: 5 MINUTES · SERVES 6–8

FOR THE COLESLAW

½ white cabbage, finely sliced

½ red cabbage, finely sliced

3 carrots, sliced into matchsticks
    (or grated if you don't have
    the patience)

1 apple, sliced into matchsticks

100g (3½oz) dry roasted peanuts

2 tablespoons black sesame seeds

seeds from 1 pomegranate

2 tablespoons chopped dill

2 tablespoons chopped chives

225g (8oz) block of halloumi
    cheese, coarsely grated

FOR THE DRESSING

3 tablespoons double cream

2 tablespoons natural yoghurt

2 tablespoons mayonnaise

1 tablespoon soy sauce

pepper

We were introduced to this recipe by our friend Nat and everybody was talking about it for weeks afterwards. Yes, it's that good. It goes with just about anything – especially in the summer – and even makes a meal on its own, thanks to the halloumi. Try it once and you'll be hooked.

Put the sliced vegetables and apple into a large bowl along with the peanuts, sesame seeds, pomegranate and most of the chopped herbs (reserving a little to garnish).

Put a frying pan on a medium heat. Add the grated halloumi to the dry pan and toast the cheese for 3–5 minutes until the pieces are golden all over. Once it's got a bit of colour, set the halloumi aside to cool.

Make the dressing by whisking all the ingredients together. Taste and season with pepper. If it's too thick, add a little more soy sauce or a dash of water.

Pour the dressing over the salad and toss to coat. Add the halloumi and the remaining chopped herbs, toss the coleslaw again and serve.

This is perfect for any roasted or grilled meats, or one of our quiches. Try it with Sticky Barbecue Ribs (see page 52), Piri-piri Drumsticks Traybake (see page 55), Quiche Lorraine (see page 115) or any of the Galettes (see pages 119–21).

Roasted Harissa Squash Salad with Preserved Lemon and Apricot Dressing

PREP: 20 MINUTES · COOK: 1 HOUR · SERVES 4–6

1 butternut squash, peeled, deseeded
    and cut into 3cm (1¼ inch) chunks
1 × 400g (14oz) can chickpeas,
    drained and dried
1 tablespoon rapeseed oil
½ teaspoon ground cinnamon
2 teaspoons ground cumin
1 teaspoon ground coriander
3 tablespoons rose harissa paste
150g (5½oz) giant couscous
30g (1oz) fresh coriander, chopped
100g (3½oz) salad leaves (we like
    to use baby spinach or rocket)
salt and pepper

FOR THE DRESSING
50g (1¾oz) dried apricots
2 preserved lemons, deseeded
2 tablespoons red wine vinegar
2 tablespoons clear honey
3 tablespoons rapeseed oil
salt and pepper

TO SERVE
200ml (7fl oz) natural yoghurt
    (plant-based if you prefer)
1 tablespoon rose harissa paste

Sweet-and-sticky butternut squash, roasted with chickpeas and harissa, is the star of this salad that is a meal in itself. With its fruity dressing, fresh green leaves and cooling yoghurt, it's irresistibly exotic. If you want to serve it as a main meal, add warm flatbreads (see page 36) and make sure there is plenty of the harissa yoghurt.

Preheat the oven to 180°C fan/200°C/400°F/Gas Mark 6.

Place the butternut squash and chickpeas in a large roasting tray. Drizzle the oil over and toss with the dried spices and some salt and pepper. Roast in the oven for 1 hour. After 30 minutes, add the harissa paste and toss well to coat. At the end of the cooking time, the squash should be tender and golden and the chickpeas roasted. Remove from the oven and place to one side.

Meanwhile, cook the giant couscous according to the packet instructions, allowing for there to be a little bite. Drain and cool.

To make the dressing, place the apricots in a small heatproof bowl and cover with boiling water. Leave the apricots to stand for 20 minutes, then drain (reserving the water) and place in a blender. Add the preserved lemons, vinegar, honey and oil. Season well and blitz until smooth. Add a little of the apricot soaking water to loosen to a pouring consistency.

Place the couscous in a large bowl with most of the chopped coriander, reserving a little to garnish. Toss with the dressing and the salad leaves (if you don't want to use all the dressing, you can keep some for another day). Spoon the couscous onto a serving platter and top with the harissa-coated squash and chickpeas. Garnish with the remaining coriander. Spoon the yoghurt into a small bowl and swirl in the harissa to serve alongside.

Serve this with chicken or lamb dishes in the summer. Try it with Moroccan-spiced Harissa Chicken (see page 25), Moroccan-spiced Lamb Tagine (see page 112) or Stuffed Sea Bass with Fennel and Dill (see page 153).

Panzanella Salad with Crispy Capers and Croutons

PREP: 20 MINUTES · COOK: 25 MINUTES · SERVES 4–6

200g (7oz) day-old ciabatta or
    sourdough, torn into chunks
6 tablespoons olive oil
2 tablespoons baby capers, drained
1kg (2lb 4oz) tomatoes, a mix of colours
    and sizes, chopped and/or sliced
2 tablespoons red wine vinegar
½ garlic clove, crushed
1 teaspoon caster sugar
20g (¾oz) basil, leaves picked
30g (1oz) rocket
10 anchovy fillets in oil
salt and pepper

Stale bread might not sound like the secret to a sensational salad, but try panzanella and you'll never look back. Use the freshest, sweetest tomatoes you can find and embrace the salty vibrancy of the capers and anchovies, as well as the peppery tang of fresh rocket and basil leaves. It's a meal in itself or lovely alongside fish, chicken or barbecued meats.

Preheat the oven to 200°C fan/220°C/425°F/Gas Mark 7.

Place the bread on a roasting tray, drizzle over 2 tablespoons of the oil and season. Pat the capers dry with kitchen paper. Toss the capers with the bread, then place in the oven for 20–25 minutes, or until crisp and golden. Remove from the oven and allow to cool.

Meanwhile, place the tomatoes in a large bowl. In a small bowl, mix the remaining oil with the vinegar, garlic and sugar, and some salt and pepper. Tip over the tomatoes and toss together.

Tear over the basil, then add the rocket and anchovy fillets. Toss well. Add the croutons and capers, and give everything a light toss. Transfer to a large platter and serve.

This summer salad will work with almost anything! Try it with Quiche Lorraine (see page 115), Salmon Wellington (see page 149) or Rosemary and Sage Porchetta (see page 130).

Braised Red Cabbage

PREP: 15 MINUTES · COOK: 1 HOUR 5 MINUTES–1 HOUR 35 MINUTES · SERVES 6

1 red cabbage, total weight about
    800g (1lb 12oz), cut into quarters

2 tablespoons unsalted butter

1 red onion, sliced

4 juniper berries, crushed

2 bay leaves

1 Bramley apple, chopped

300ml (10fl oz) red wine

50ml (2fl oz) red or white wine vinegar

50g (1¾oz) light soft brown sugar

salt and pepper

Sweet, tangy, slow-cooked red cabbage is a staple in our freezers through autumn and winter. It brightens up any plate and is particularly good with casseroles and roasts (and essential on Christmas Day). You won't regret making a bigger batch than you need, as it freezes brilliantly and can be speedily reheated in the microwave.

To prepare the cabbage, cut out the core from each quarter and thinly slice the cabbage. Place in a colander and rinse under cold running water.

Place a large saucepan or casserole dish on a medium heat and add the butter. When it has melted, add the onion, juniper berries and bay leaves. Fry for 5 minutes, or until the onion starts to soften.

Stir in the cabbage, followed by the apple, wine, vinegar and sugar. Season, then cover with a lid. Bring to the boil, then reduce to a low simmer and cook for 1–1½ hours, stirring occasionally, or until the cabbage is softened and looking glossy. Top up with a little water if needed. Season to taste and serve hot.

Creamed Spinach

PREP: 10 MINUTES · COOK: 10 MINUTES · SERVES 6–8

500g (1lb 2oz) spinach

30g (1oz) unsalted butter

3 garlic cloves, sliced

2 shallots, finely chopped

300ml (10fl oz) single cream

a little grated nutmeg

a squeeze of lemon juice

salt and pepper

Such a decadent way to serve spinach, this is great with roasts, steak and fish. Elevate by spooning the creamed spinach into a baking dish, topping with breadcrumbs and grated Parmesan cheese, and grilling until golden.

Place the spinach in a colander, pour boiling water over and allow to wilt. When cool enough to handle, press through the colander to remove as much liquid as possible. Finely chop the spinach, transfer to a bowl and place to one side.

Place a large frying pan on a low heat. Add the butter, then stir in the garlic and shallots. Cook for about 5 minutes until softened. Add the cream and stir – it will take about 5 minutes to achieve a smooth, lump-free sauce.

Stir in the spinach along with a few gratings of nutmeg and a squeeze of lemon juice. Season to taste and serve.

Cauliflower Cheese

PREP: 15 MINUTES · COOK: 40 MINUTES · SERVES 4–6

FOR THE SAUCE

50g (1¾oz) unsalted butter,
   plus extra for greasing

500ml (18fl oz) milk

2 garlic cloves, crushed

50g (1¾oz) plain flour

1 tablespoon Dijon mustard

100g (3½oz) vintage Cheddar
   cheese, grated

FOR THE ROASTED CAULIFLOWER

1 cauliflower, total weight about 650g
   (1lb 7oz), broken into florets (with
   half the stalk sliced too – optional)

2 tablespoons olive oil

salt and pepper

FOR THE TOPPING

20g (¾oz) fresh breadcrumbs

20g (¾oz) Parmesan cheese, grated

a few parsley sprigs, leaves picked
   and chopped

salt and pepper

*This is delicious on its own but is also a
great side for chicken or beef. Try it with
Huntsman's Chicken (see page 142),
Beef Wellington (see pages 139–40) or
Nut Roast with Balsamic Red Onions
(see page 154).*

A no-holds-barred version of the comforting classic that can definitely be a main course, not just a side dish. Roasting the cauliflower first brings a lovely nutty taste and a much better texture (it also removes the moisture – essential if you're going to make extra to freeze). There was widespread rejoicing from our shop teams when we started making this a few years ago – they'd been asking for it for ages.

Preheat the oven to 180°C fan/200°C/400°F/Gas Mark 6. Grease a 20 × 25cm (8 × 10 inch) ovenproof dish.

Place the cauliflower florets in a roasting tray, drizzle with half of the olive oil, season, then roast in the oven for 30 minutes until tender and starting to turn golden.

Meanwhile, if you're using the cauliflower stalk slices, add these to a food processor and blitz to the consistency of couscous. Tip out onto a baking tray, drizzle with the remaining oil, season and roast in the oven for 20 minutes to dry out.

While the cauliflower is roasting, gently heat the milk in a heatproof jug in the microwave or in a saucepan on the hob. Place a medium saucepan on a low heat and add the butter. When it has melted, add the garlic and cook for 1 minute, stirring, making sure the garlic doesn't colour. Stir in the flour. Cook, still stirring, for 2 minutes, or until the paste is golden and bubbling. Using a ladle, gradually add the warm milk, whisking between each addition to form a thin, smooth sauce. Stir in the mustard and Cheddar and remove from the heat. Season to taste.

In a small bowl, mix together the breadcrumbs, Parmesan and parsley with a pinch of salt and pepper.

Once the cauliflower is roasted, remove from the oven. Preheat the grill to low/medium. Tip the florets into the prepared dish.

If you're using the blitzed stalk, add 3 tablespoons of the cauliflower crumbs to the breadcrumb mix and stir to combine. Place the rest of the blitzed stalk in the dish with the florets. Pour the sauce over the cauliflower and sprinkle over the breadcrumb mix. Place the dish under the grill, on the middle shelf if possible, for about 10 minutes until bubbling and golden. Keep an eye on it to make sure it doesn't burn. Allow to sit for 2 minutes before serving.

Dauphinoise Potatoes

PREP: 20 MINUTES · COOK: 1 HOUR 15 MINUTES · SERVES 6

50g (1¾oz) unsalted butter, plus extra
    for greasing and dotting on top
600ml (20fl oz) double cream
5 garlic cloves, sliced
10 thyme sprigs
6–8 large Maris Piper potatoes,
    total weight 1–1.25kg (2lb 4oz–
    2lb 12oz), peeled
a little grated nutmeg
100g (3½oz) vintage Cheddar
    cheese, grated
salt and pepper

Butter, garlic, cream, potatoes, cheese – how can any combination of these ingredients be anything other than absurdly comforting and moreish? Here we have layers of soft, garlic-infused potatoes, basking in butter and cream, hidden beneath a golden, cheesy topping. Feel free to mix up your cheeses – Parmesan, Gruyère and Comté all work well. You could even try adding some Stilton for a bolder flavour.

Grease a 20 × 25cm (8 × 10 inch) ovenproof dish with butter. Season the dish.

Place the cream, garlic and thyme sprigs in a medium saucepan on a low heat. Allow the cream to steam gently (not boil) for about 5 minutes to allow the flavours to infuse. Remove from the heat.

Using a mandoline, the slicing attachment on the food processor or a sharp chef's knife, slice the potatoes as thinly as possible.

Preheat the oven to 170°C fan/190°C/375°F/Gas Mark 5.

Strain the cream through a sieve into a jug, keeping the thyme sprigs and garlic. Layer some of the potatoes in the prepared dish until the potatoes are two to three layers deep. Season and add a few gratings of nutmeg, a few dots of butter, a few slices of the reserved garlic and a few picked thyme leaves. Repeat the layering until you've used up all of the sliced potato. Pour over the cream and scatter the cheese on top. Cover the dish tightly with a piece of buttered tin foil and place in the oven for 40 minutes.

Remove the foil and cook for a further 20–30 minutes until the dish is golden and the potatoes are cooked through. Allow to sit for 5 minutes, then serve.

This is a wonderful side for most beef, chicken or lamb dishes. Try it with Beef Bourguignon (see page 84), Coq au Vin (see page 100) or Rosemary and Sage Porchetta (see page 130).

'Finish your meal as you mean life to go on; sweet and moreish'

– COOK

KITCHEN WISDOM NO.6

You Deserve Pudding!

Life is sweet and the ending to
a great meal should be too.

Here's the pick of the puds from our
award-winning Somerset kitchen.

PUDDINGS KNOW-HOW

On the edge of the village of Ilton in Somerset, looking out over fields towards the Blackdown Hills, you'll find COOK Puddings. We often call it our Willy Wonka kitchen. Stand on the stairway looking down into the big room where everybody is busy whipping, mixing, rolling, baking and decorating, with a sweet, creamy aroma filling the air, and you'll appreciate why.

Its roots go back to the late 1990s and the kitchen of Liz Dove's suburban Surrey home. To bring in some extra money for her young family, Liz started baking puddings to be frozen and sold in the nearby Priory Farm Shop – chocolate roulade, fruit vacherin and lemon cheesecake.

These puddings caught the attention of COOK co-founder, Ed, who asked Liz if we could sell them in our first two shops. As COOK grew, so Liz needed a bigger kitchen. First she expanded into her garage, then to a farm in Somerset, where she converted the cowsheds. Eventually, she even outgrew those. So, in 2015, we opened the purpose-built COOK Puddings nearby.

Liz has since retired, entrusting the running of the kitchen to Sarah and Danni, a mother-and-daughter team who have been with us for years. And while the size of the kitchen has changed since Liz first started, the pudding recipes, and the way we make them, remain the same. Give them a go – few things spread joy like a big pud.

Some pudding-making advice from Liz

All of these recipes can easily be doubled up –
and also made in a bigger or deeper tin.

Most recipes are adaptable to whatever fruit or
flavour combinations you like – treat the basic recipe
as a blank canvas.

Make sure you have a nice flat plate/platter to serve from – any
ridges around the edges of your plates will ruin all your hard work.

Dusting with icing sugar elevates the look of just about any pudding and
disguises any cracks or blemishes on the surface. This is particularly helpful
for roulades and pavlovas, which invariably crack when you roll them.

For sophisticated, neat slices, it's essential for the pudding to be cold – the
warmer it gets, the more difficult slicing becomes. But make sure you use
a hot knife blade to cut. Keep a jug of recently boiled water to hand to rinse
off the blade in between each slice.

Rolled Pavlovas

PREP: 45 MINUTES, PLUS CHILLING · COOK: 40 MINUTES–1 HOUR · SERVES 6–8

FOR EACH MERINGUE
35g (1¼oz) cornflour
45ml (3 tablespoons) white
    wine vinegar
30ml (2 tablespoons) vanilla extract
5 egg whites
250g (9oz) caster sugar
icing sugar, for dusting

Our award-winning rolled pavlovas are renowned and we've picked four classic combinations to get you started. When it comes to rolling, fortune favours the bold. Be decisive when you tip out the meringue and then bold with your roll – just go for it. Use the parchment or greaseproof paper to help you roll. If it doesn't quite work, so be it – it will still taste great.

Chocolate and Amaretti Pavlova

meringue ingredients, as above
25g (¾oz) cocoa powder, sifted,
    plus extra to serve
25g (¾oz) amaretti biscuits, crushed
250ml (9fl oz) whipping cream
1 tablespoon cold espresso coffee
½ tablespoon brandy (optional)
a little grated chocolate (optional)

Make the meringue following the method on page 190 but adding the cocoa powder to the sugar. When you've finished the meringue mix, stir in the crushed amaretti biscuits and then cook as described on page 190. Remove from the oven and allow to cool at room temperature for about 30 minutes.

Whip the cream to soft peaks. Mix the cold coffee with the brandy (if using).

Assemble the pavlova roll as described on page 190, spreading with the cream and spooning over the coffee (and brandy). Carefully transfer the pavlova roll to a serving plate or board, making sure the crease is at the bottom. Cover loosely with clingfilm and chill in the fridge for 2–4 hours. If you leave it for longer or overnight, it will become quite sticky.

To serve, dust with a little cocoa powder or a sprinkling of grated chocolate.

When whipping cream for a pavlova, you're aiming for it to hold still on a spoon or spatula, then slowly fall off. For a lighter, less sweet pudding, swap the cream for whipped crème fraîche, mascarpone or a mix of half Greek yoghurt, half cream.

Cherry and Blackberry Pavlova

100g (3½oz) cherries, fresh or frozen,
   stones removed

100g (3½oz) blackberries, fresh
   or frozen

2 tablespoons caster sugar

juice of 1 lemon

1 teaspoon cornflour

meringue ingredients (see page 189)

250ml (9fl oz) whipping cream

First, make the filling. Place the fruit in a small saucepan along with the sugar, lemon juice and cornflour. Place on a low heat and gently poach the fruit for about 10 minutes until just cooked and the sauce has thickened. Remove from the heat and place to one side.

Now make the meringue. Line a 25cm × 35cm (10 × 14 inch) Swiss roll tin with nonstick baking paper. In a small bowl, mix together the cornflour, vinegar and vanilla extract, then place to one side.

Preheat the oven to 160°C fan/180°C/350°F/Gas Mark 4.

Place the egg whites in a free-standing mixer with a whisk attachment, or use a large mixing bowl and an electric hand whisk. Whisk the egg whites until stiff and holding their shape. Whisk in half of the cornflour mix until just combined. Next, whisk in half of the sugar until combined. Add the rest of the sugar and cornflour mix, and whisk in thoroughly. Spoon the mixture into the prepared tin and gently level out with a palette knife. Bake in the oven for about 40 minutes, or until set. Remove from the oven and allow to cool at room temperature for about 30 minutes.

When the meringue has cooled, whip the cream to soft peaks. Turn the meringue out onto a clean tea towel so that the top of the meringue is face down. Gently remove the baking paper. With the shorter edge facing you, score a horizontal line 1cm (½ inch) in from the edge to assist with rolling. Spread the whipped cream over the meringue and drizzle over 2 tablespoons of the fruit sauce. Spoon the fruit over in an even layer. From the short edge facing you, carefully roll the meringue away from you into a spiral, making sure you don't create a triangle shape. Use the tea towel to help you roll. Don't worry if the meringue cracks.

Carefully transfer the pavlova roll to a serving plate or board, making sure the crease is at the bottom. Cover loosely with clingfilm and chill in the fridge for 2–4 hours. If you leave it for longer or overnight, it will become quite sticky.

When you're ready to serve, dust the pavlova roll with a little icing sugar and slice.

Raspberry Pavlova

150g (5½oz) fresh raspberries
1 tablespoon caster sugar
2 tablespoons lemon juice
½ teaspoon cornflour
meringue ingredients (see page 189)
250ml (9fl oz) whipping cream

In the beginning there was raspberry pav... To make the original COOK pavlova, put 100g (3½oz) of the raspberries in a small saucepan with the sugar and lemon juice. Cook on a low heat until the fruit is soft but still holding its shape. Strain the fruit into a bowl and return the juice to the pan. Add the cornflour and stir on a low heat until the sauce is thickened but still runny. Remove from the heat and place to one side to cool.

Lightly crush the remaining raspberries.

Make and cook the meringue and whip the cream as described in the recipe opposite. Assemble the pavlova roll in the same way, spreading with the cream, then the cooked and fresh raspberries and the sauce. Chill in the same way. To serve, dust with icing sugar.

Cinnamon and Autumn Fruit Pavlova

1 eating apple, finely chopped
150g (5½oz) frozen berries
2 tablespoons caster sugar
1 teaspoon ground cinnamon,
    plus a little more for dusting
2 tablespoons lemon juice
½ teaspoon cornflour
meringue ingredients (see page 189)
250ml (9fl oz) whipping cream

Place the apple in a small saucepan with the berries, sugar, half of the ground cinnamon and the lemon juice. Cook on a low heat for about 20 minutes, or until the fruit is soft but still holding its shape. Strain the fruit into a bowl and return the juice to the pan. Add the cornflour and stir on a low heat until the sauce is thickened but still runny. Remove from the heat and place to one side to cool.

Make and cook the meringue as described in the recipe opposite, adding the remaining ground cinnamon to the cornflour, vinegar and vanilla extract mixture for the meringue. Whip the cream to soft peaks. Assemble the pavlova roll in the same way, spreading with the cinnamon cream, then the autumnal fruits and the sauce. Chill in the same way. To serve, dust with icing sugar mixed with a little cinnamon.

Chocolate and Raspberry Roulade

PREP: 35 MINUTES · COOK: 1 HOUR · SERVES 6–8

30g (1oz) unsalted butter,
  plus extra for greasing
150g (5½oz) dark chocolate
  (at least 53% cocoa solids),
  chopped into pieces
100ml (3½fl oz) warm water
6 eggs, separated
225g (8oz) caster sugar
250ml (9fl oz) whipping cream
1–2 tablespoons icing sugar,
  for dusting and serving
200g (7oz) fresh raspberries,
  plus extra for serving

Soft chocolate sponge, whipped cream, raspberries... Pudding (and life) doesn't get much better than this. If raspberries aren't your thing though, just leave them out or add in the fruit of your choice. COOK Puddings founder Liz started making the original recipe when working as a chalet girl in her early twenties and it never failed to get a round of applause. So when she started making frozen puddings to sell in her local farm shop, it was her go-to recipe. The raspberries were added one Christmas as a bit of a festive flourish and have stuck ever since. You can bake the sponge a day ahead, so you only need to fill and roll just before serving.

Preheat the oven to 160°C fan/180°C/350°F/Gas Mark 4. Grease and line a 25cm × 35cm (10 × 14 inch) Swiss roll tin with nonstick baking paper.

Place the chocolate in a small saucepan with the measured water. Place on a low heat. Stir until the chocolate has melted. Remove from the heat and allow to cool for 5 minutes. Stir in the butter and allow it to melt in the residual heat.

Place the egg yolks and sugar in a free-standing mixer with a whisk attachment, or use a large mixing bowl and an electric hand whisk. Whisk for about 8 minutes until pale. Fold in the chocolate, then transfer to another bowl and put to one side. Wash and dry the bowl and the whisk attachment or electric hand whisk thoroughly – any grease in the bowl will prevent the egg whites whisking properly. Add the egg whites to the bowl and whisk to soft peaks. Fold in the chocolate mixture. Spoon the roulade mixture into the prepared tin and gently level out with a spatula. Bake in the oven for 55 minutes, or until the roulade has risen. Remove from the oven and allow to cool completely at room temperature.

When the sponge has cooled, whip the cream to soft peaks. Carefully turn the sponge out onto a clean tea towel dusted with icing sugar so that the top of the sponge is facing down. Gently remove the baking paper. With the shorter edge facing you, score a horizontal line 1cm (½ inch) in from the edge to assist with rolling. Spread the whipped cream evenly over the sponge, right up to the edges. Scatter the raspberries over in an even layer. From the short edge facing you, carefully roll the sponge away from you into a spiral. Use the tea towel to help you roll. You can apply a bit of pressure as you roll to get a more rounded shape. Don't worry if it cracks as you roll.

Carefully transfer the roulade to a serving plate or board. Dust with icing sugar, slice and serve with extra raspberries.

It's easier to cut neat slices if the roulade is cold, so keep it on its serving plate in the fridge until just before you serve. If you're unhappy with anything less than perfection, freeze the roulade, slice while frozen, then transfer to individual plates to thaw. Some extra cream, served alongside or poured over, is a nice touch.

Vanilla Cheesecake

PREP: 45 MINUTES, PLUS OVERNIGHT CHILLING · COOK: 5–30 MINUTES · SERVES 6–8

FOR THE BASE
125g (4½oz) unsalted butter,
    plus extra for greasing
225g (8oz) digestive biscuits

FOR THE FILLING
250ml (9fl oz) whipping cream
280g (10oz) cream cheese
1 tablespoon vanilla bean paste
50g (1¾oz) icing sugar, sifted

An endlessly adaptable cheesecake recipe that's virtually foolproof. As well as the classic vanilla version, we've picked a couple of our favourite flavour combinations from the COOK archives, but do stir whatever you fancy through the filling – melted chocolate, salted caramel or toffee are all obvious alternatives to fruit.

Grease the inside and line the base of a 20cm (8 inch) springform cake tin with a circle of nonstick baking paper.

Place the butter in a saucepan on a low heat and allow to melt. Place the digestive biscuits in a large freezer bag and bash to sand-like crumbs with a rolling pin. Alternatively, you could blitz the biscuits in a food processor. Tip into the pan of melted butter and stir. Spoon into the prepared cake tin, spreading it out evenly and pressing down well with the back of the spoon to form a firm base. Place in the fridge for at least 30 minutes to set.

Whip the cream to soft peaks in a large bowl. Place the cream cheese and vanilla bean paste in a separate large mixing bowl and beat with the icing sugar until smooth. Fold in the whipped cream. Spoon the mixture onto the base and level out with a spatula. Place in the fridge, lightly covered with clingfilm, for at least 4 hours but preferably overnight, to set.

When ready to serve, run a warm knife around the sides of the cheesecake to help ease it out. Slice and serve.

ELDERFLOWER AND STRAWBERRY
To make a refreshing summer cheesecake for an al fresco meal, add elderflower cordial and strawberries. When preparing the tin, line the inside of the tin with a layer of sliced strawberries to decorate the outside of the cheesecake – sit the slices on the base, flat against the side of the tin. Make and chill the biscuit base and whip the cream as above. Add 3 tablespoons elderflower cordial to the filling with the icing sugar. Make a sauce with 100g (3½oz) chopped strawberries, a splash of elderflower cordial and a squeeze of lemon juice – blitz with a hand blender, then pass through a sieve. Discard the juice and fold the pulp through the filling mixture before spreading over the base. Chill to set as above. Decorate with more sliced strawberries on top.

For a lighter pudding, swap the cream for fromage frais.

CLASSIC LEMON

Use a good-quality lemon curd to make a zingy lemony version. Make and chill the biscuit base and whip the cream as on page 195. Replace the vanilla paste with 2 tablespoons lemon juice and add the zest of 3 lemons to the cream cheese and icing sugar to make the filling. Stir 4 tablespoons lemon curd into the filling before folding in the whipped cream (make sure the cream is only whipped to soft peaks – the lemon causes the cream to thicken again, so you need to be careful it's not overwhipped). When it's in the tin, swirl in 2 tablespoons lemon curd (loosened with a little lemon juice if it's a bit thick) and sprinkle over the zest of 2 more lemons. Chill to set as on page 195.

WHITE CHOCOLATE AND RASPBERRY

For a decadent and very pretty chocolate and raspberry cheesecake, first make a quick raspberry coulis by blitzing 100g (3½oz) raspberries with a hand blender. Set this to one side while you make and chill the biscuit base and whip the cream as on page 195. Melt 85g (3oz) white chocolate with 3 tablespoons double cream in a heatproof bowl over a pan of gently simmering water. Fold this into the cheesecake filling before you assemble the cheesecake. Spread half of the filling mixture over the base, then scatter over 50g (1¾oz) fresh raspberries. Spoon the rest of the filling on top, level it out with a spatula, then drop spoonfuls of the raspberry coulis in a pattern on top of the cheesecake and use a cocktail stick, the end of a skewer or the tip of a teaspoon to make some little swirls. Chill to set as on page 195.

RHUBARB AND GINGER

For a delicious spiced version, replace the digestive biscuits in the base with ginger nut biscuits. Chop 2 balls of stem ginger in syrup and add to the biscuit mix. Make and chill the biscuit base. Chop 2 rhubarb sticks (total weight about 150g/5½oz) and add to a saucepan with 50g (1¾oz) fresh or frozen raspberries, the zest of 1 orange, 2 tablespoons caster sugar and 2 tablespoons water. Cook on a low heat for 20–30 minutes until softened and cooked. Strain through a sieve, pushing the pulp through and leaving the seeds behind. Put this thick sauce to one side to cool. Whip the cream and assemble the cheesecake as on page 195. Swirl the cooled fruit sauce through the topping. Chill to set as on page 195.

Baked Cheesecake

PREP: 25 MINUTES · COOK: 1 HOUR 30 MINUTES · SERVES 6–8

FOR THE BASE

125g (4½oz) butter, plus extra
    for greasing
60g (2¼oz) caster sugar
140g (5oz) plain flour
30g (1oz) semolina

FOR THE FILLING

420g (14oz) full-fat cream cheese
150g (5½oz) caster sugar
grated zest of 2 lemons
300ml (10½fl oz) soured cream
2 eggs
1½ teaspoons vanilla bean paste
125g (4½oz) blueberries (optional)
icing sugar, to decorate

*Instead of the shortbread base, you
can use the digestive biscuit base from
the Vanilla Cheesecake (see page 195),
if you prefer.*

A fantastically simple, New York-style cheesecake – rich, dense and creamy. It's delicious just as it is but, if you want to add fruit, blueberries are the best to bake into it, as they don't tend to bleed their colour. Otherwise, wait until the cheesecake has cooled and add whatever fruit or decoration you like on top – sliced strawberries in a concentric pattern look very pretty.

Preheat the oven to 160°C fan/180°C/350°F/Gas Mark 4. Lightly grease and line a 20cm (8 inch) loose-bottomed or springform cake tin.

To make the base, put all the ingredients into a food processor and blitz until the mixture resembles breadcrumbs. Alternatively, you can cream the butter and sugar together by hand, then add the flour and semolina to make a grainy crumb texture. Press the biscuit mix into the prepared tin, spreading it out evenly and pressing it down with the back of the spoon to form a firm base. Don't worry if it starts to push up the sides a little. Cook the base in the oven for 35 minutes. Remove from the oven and allow to cool.

Reduce the oven temperature to 140°C fan/160°C/325°F/Gas Mark 3.

To make the filling, place the cream cheese, sugar and lemon zest in a large mixing bowl and beat until smooth. Fold in the soured cream until just combined. Whisk the eggs with the vanilla bean paste, then fold into the cream cheese mixture – make sure there are no lumps. Spoon the mixture onto the base and level out with a spatula.

Place the cheesecake in the oven and bake for 50–55 minutes until set.

Allow to cool before serving, sprinkled with blueberries (if using) and dusted with icing sugar.

Fruit Vacherin

PREP: 45 MINUTES · COOK: 1 HOUR 15 MINUTES · SERVES 10–12

FOR THE MERINGUE
5 egg whites
250g (9oz) caster sugar
20g (¾oz) skinned hazelnuts,
    toasted and chopped

FOR THE COULIS
200g (7oz) mix of berries –
    we like raspberries, strawberries,
    redcurrants and blueberries

FOR THE FILLING AND TOPPING
400g (14oz) seasonal berries
450ml (16fl oz) whipping cream

FOR GARNISH (OPTIONAL)
20g (¾oz) hazelnuts, toasted
    and chopped
20g (¾oz) pistachios, chopped
10g (¼oz) dried raspberries
thyme sprigs

Make sure you spread the fruit and cream filling right up to the edges of the meringue so you get everything showing on each layer. It doesn't matter if it dribbles over the side – that's all part of the charm.

A flamboyant, multi-layered meringue that you can build as high as you dare. The version we sell is fully covered in cream for the very simple reason that, if you're sending multi-layered meringues around the country, they tend to get bashed and broken and not look particularly impressive when they arrive – a blanket of cream was the answer!

Preheat the oven to 130°C fan/150°C/300°F/Gas Mark 2. Cut three pieces of baking paper and, using a pencil, draw a 23cm (9 inch) circle on each piece. Place the pieces of baking paper on three baking trays.

Place the egg whites in a free-standing mixer with a whisk attachment, or use a large clean mixing bowl and an electric hand whisk. Whisk until stiff. Add half of the sugar and whisk again until very stiff. Add the remaining sugar. Whisk until just incorporated. Take about one-third of the mixture and pipe or spread the meringue onto one of the baking-paper circles. Gently fold the chopped hazelnuts into the remaining meringue. Pipe or spread the hazelnut meringue onto the remaining two baking-paper circles. Place the three baking trays into the oven for 1¼ hours, or until the meringue is completely dry. Turn the oven off and allow to cool in the oven with the door open. Make sure the meringue is completely cool before you start assembling.

Meanwhile, make the coulis. Using an electric whisk, whizz the berries until you make a purée. Push the purée through a sieve to remove all the seeds so that you have a smooth sauce.

When you are ready to assemble the vacherin, chop 250g (9oz) of the seasonal berries into small pieces, leaving the rest whole. Whip the cream into soft peaks. Place one of the hazelnut meringue discs onto your serving dish. Cover with one-third of the whipped cream. Drizzle 1–2 tablespoons of the coulis over the cream. Scatter half of the chopped fruit over the coulis and cream, spreading the filling out as flat as possible and taking it right to the edges. Repeat using the plain meringue disc, another third of whipped cream, a little more coulis and the rest of the chopped fruit. Top with the remaining hazelnut meringue disc. Spread the last third of the whipped cream over the meringue and arrange the whole fruit on top. Scatter over the hazelnuts, pistachios, dried raspberries, or thyme sprigs (if using).

If you have time, place in the fridge for a couple of hours (but no more!) before serving, to allow the cream to soften the meringue a little. This makes slicing and serving the meringue easier but is not essential.

Apricot, Orange and Almond Torte

PREP: 15 MINUTES · COOK: 45 MINUTES · SERVES 4–6

90g (3¼oz) coconut oil, melted, plus extra for greasing

175g (6oz) gluten-free self-raising flour

100g (3½oz) ground almonds

125g (4½oz) caster sugar

½ teaspoon gluten-free baking powder

150ml (5fl oz) soya milk or other plant-based milk

1 drop almond extract (optional)

1 tablespoon white wine vinegar

grated zest of 1 orange

40g (1½oz) fine cornmeal polenta or 30g (1oz) fresh breadcrumbs

6 apricot halves, canned or fresh, stones removed

10g (¼oz) flaked almonds, plus a few extra, toasted, to serve

crème fraîche, to serve (optional)

FOR THE SYRUP

70g (2½oz) caster sugar

grated zest and juice of ½ orange

This is something of a miracle pudding-cum-cake in that it ticks virtually every box in terms of dietary preferences (it's vegan and gluten- and dairy-free) and still manages to delight everybody when it comes to taste. Serving it warm is pretty much essential. If you have leftovers or have made the torte ahead of time, heating each slice for 20 seconds in the microwave will do the trick. If apricots aren't your thing, just swap in another stone fruit or berry.

Preheat the oven to 170°C fan/190°C/375°F/Gas Mark 5. Grease and line a 20cm (8 inch) round cake tin with coconut oil.

Place the flour, ground almonds, sugar and baking powder in a bowl and mix. Place the melted coconut oil, milk, almond extract (if using), vinegar and orange zest in a separate large mixing bowl. Slowly stir the flour mixture into the liquid mixture until combined, then fold in the polenta or breadcrumbs.

Spoon the mixture into the prepared cake tin. Top with the apricot halves, cut-sides down, and sprinkle over the flaked almonds. Bake in the oven for 45 minutes, or until risen and golden.

Meanwhile, make the syrup. Place the sugar in a small saucepan along with the orange zest and juice and 2 tablespoons of water. Heat for 2–3 minutes until reduced by half. Remove from the heat.

When the cake is ready, remove it from the oven and place the tin on a wire rack. Prick about 20 holes in the cake with a cocktail stick (avoiding the apricots) and spoon over the warm syrup. Allow to cool in the tin, then turn it out onto a wire rack to cool a little more – not for too long though, as the torte is best served warm. Serve with crème fraîche (if you want) and a few extra toasted flaked almonds.

You can make a simple apricot coulis to serve alongside: cook 6 dried apricots with 1 tablespoon of sugar and just enough water to cover the fruit on a low heat for about 10 minutes, then blitz to a purée in a food processor.

Chocolate and Pear Fondant Pudding

PREP: 25 MINUTES · COOK: 30 MINUTES · SERVES 4–6

50g (1¾oz) unsalted butter, plus extra
   for greasing
1 × 410g (14oz) can pear quarters, drained
50g (1¾oz) amaretti biscuits, crushed to
   a chunky breadcrumb texture
60ml (4 tablespoons) double cream
125g (4½oz) dark chocolate (at least 70%
   cocoa solids), chopped into pieces
3 eggs
70g (2½oz) caster sugar
cream or ice cream, to serve

The simplest, most satisfying and easiest-to-adapt recipe that you can whip up in a flash. During lockdown, we did a brilliant live, online cook-a-long with Liz making this. You can eat it when it's warm and gooey. Or let it cool so it's more like a brownie. Or ditch the baking altogether and eat it straight from the fridge or freezer, like a mousse or parfait. If you don't want to use pears, add whatever fruit you like … or none at all. You can even put fruit at one end of the tin and leave the other end plain, for the fussy kids (grown-up ones included).

Preheat the oven to 160°C fan/180°C/350°F/Gas Mark 4. Grease a 20cm (8 inch) cake or brownie tin with butter.

Arrange the pear pieces in the base of the prepared tin and sprinkle over the amaretti biscuits.

Place the butter, cream and chocolate in a medium saucepan. Place on a low heat, stirring, for 3–5 minutes until the chocolate has just melted. If you have a kitchen thermometer, you can test the temperature – don't let it get hotter than 50°C (122°F). Remove from the heat and leave to cool.

Place the eggs and sugar in a free-standing mixer with a whisk attachment, or use a large mixing bowl and an electric hand whisk. Whisk until thick and the beaters leave a trail when you lift the whisk up.

With a metal spoon, fold the egg mixture into the cooled chocolate mixture until just combined. Pour this mixture over the pears and biscuits in the prepared tin and bake in the oven for 20–25 minutes until just set but still oozy, with a lovely glazed, slightly cracked top. Serve immediately with cream or ice cream.

You could also serve extra pear halves or slices and more crushed amaretti biscuits on the side.

Chocolate and Hazelnut Parfait

PREP: 30 MINUTES, PLUS 4 HOURS CHILLING · COOK: 1 HOUR 5 MINUTES · SERVES 6–8

FOR THE HAZELNUT MERINGUE

5 egg whites

275g (9¾oz) caster sugar

½ teaspoon vanilla extract

1 teaspoon cornflour

100g (3½oz) blanched hazelnuts,
    toasted and chopped

FOR THE CHOCOLATE SAUCE

100g (3½oz) dark chocolate
    (at least 70% cocoa solids),
    chopped into pieces

2 tablespoons roasted hazelnut
    syrup (optional)

TO ASSEMBLE

450ml (16fl oz) whipping cream

100g (3½oz) blanched hazelnuts,
    toasted and chopped

If you're short of time, or just can't help yourself, you can serve the parfait without freezing – it will be more like a heavy mousse. Just spoon into a big trifle bowl or individual bowls and decorate with the remaining chopped meringue, chocolate sauce and hazelnuts.

Another endlessly adaptable recipe, this time inherited from Liz's mum, who would make it in a round pudding bowl as a chocolate bombe – a great alternative to Christmas pudding. You can make it boozy by stirring a tablespoon or two of your favourite spirit through the cream – try marsala, sherry, whisky, Cointreau…

Start by making the meringue. Preheat the oven to 130°C fan/150°C/300°F/ Gas Mark 2. Line both a baking sheet and a 20cm (8 inch) loose-bottomed cake tin with nonstick baking paper.

Place the egg whites in a free-standing mixer, or use a large mixing bowl an electric hand whisk. Beat until stiff peaks are formed, then add the sugar, one-quarter at a time, beating well for 1 minute between each addition until glossy, thick and holding its shape. Beat in the vanilla extract and cornflour until thoroughly incorporated. Fold in the chopped hazelnuts. Spread the mixture evenly over the baking sheet so you have a meringue about 2cm (¾ inch) high. Bake in the oven for 1 hour until lightly golden and set. Allow to cool in the oven with the door open. Once the meringue is cool, chop it into large chunks.

Now make the chocolate sauce. Place the chocolate and 40ml (3 tablespoons) water in a heatproof bowl over a pan of gently simmering water. Heat for about 2 minutes, stirring well, until combined and smooth. Stir in the syrup (if using), then place to one side to cool at room temperature.

Lightly whip the cream in a large mixing bowl. Fold in most of the chopped meringue, half of the chocolate sauce and half of the chopped, toasted hazelnuts.

To assemble the parfait, spoon the chocolate cream mixture into the prepared cake tin. Top with the remaining chopped meringue, drizzle over the rest of the chocolate sauce and sprinkle over the remaining hazelnuts. Cover with clingfilm and place in the freezer for about 4 hours to set.

Before serving, remove from the tin and place on your serving dish, then let stand at room temperature for about 1½ hours. If it's a very warm day, you could do this in the fridge. Cut into slices and serve.

Gin and Tonic Semifreddo

PREP: 40 MINUTES, PLUS OVERNIGHT CHILLING · SERVES 6

FOR THE PARFAIT
2 egg whites
100g (3½oz) caster sugar
250ml (9fl oz) whipping cream
45ml (3 tablespoons) gin of choice
2 tablespoons lemon juice
grated zest of 1 lemon
grated zest of 1 lime

FOR THE LEMON SWIRL
40g (1½oz) lemon curd
1 teaspoon gin of your choice
1 teaspoon tonic water (optional)

FOR THE TOPPING
grated zest of 1 lime
grated zest of 1 lemon

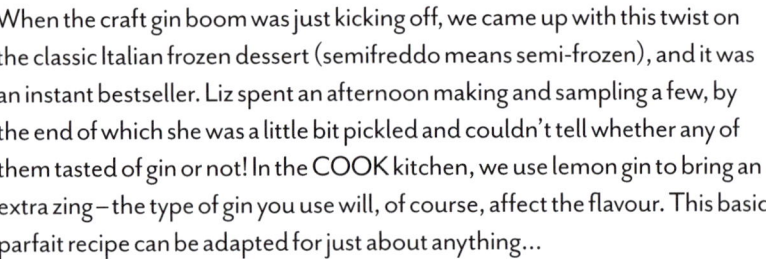

When the craft gin boom was just kicking off, we came up with this twist on the classic Italian frozen dessert (semifreddo means semi-frozen), and it was an instant bestseller. Liz spent an afternoon making and sampling a few, by the end of which she was a little bit pickled and couldn't tell whether any of them tasted of gin or not! In the COOK kitchen, we use lemon gin to bring an extra zing – the type of gin you use will, of course, affect the flavour. This basic parfait recipe can be adapted for just about anything…

Line a 1 litre (1¾ pint) loaf tin with clingfilm.

Place the egg whites in a free-standing mixer with a whisk attachment, or use a large mixing bowl and an electric hand whisk. Whisk the egg whites until stiff peaks are formed, then add the sugar, one-quarter at a time, beating well for 1 minute between each addition until glossy, thick and holding its shape.

In a separate bowl, lightly whip the cream to very soft peaks (be careful not to overwhip as the cream will thicken more when the lemon juice is added). Fold in the gin, lemon juice and lemon and lime zest. Gently fold the cream into the meringue mix. Spoon the mixture into the prepared tin.

In a small bowl, mix together the lemon swirl ingredients. Spoon little blobs over the parfait and use the tip of a teaspoon to swirl in a pattern. Scatter the lime and lemon zest over the top.

Cover the parfait lightly with clingfilm and place in the freezer overnight. Either serve straight from the freezer or allow the parfait to sit at room temperature for 10 minutes first. Slice and serve.

At COOK Puddings, everybody has their own decorating technique and style.
A good place to begin is to swirl figures of eight or backwards sixes. A little bit
of practice and you'll soon get the knack.

Pear and Ginger Tart

PREP: 45 MINUTES, PLUS CHILLING · COOK: 1 HOUR 15 MINUTES · SERVES 6–8

FOR THE PASTRY

100g (3½oz) butter, plus extra
    for greasing
225g (8oz) plain flour, plus extra
    for dusting
50g (1¾oz) icing sugar
1 egg

FOR THE FRANGIPANE

125g (4½oz) unsalted butter, softened,
    at room temperature
125g (4½oz) caster sugar
2 eggs, beaten, at room temperature
70g (2½oz) plain flour
70g (2½oz) ground almonds
2 drops almond extract

FOR THE TOPPING

70g (2½oz) stem ginger in syrup,
    chopped
250g (9oz) canned pears, drained
    and quartered
10g (¼oz) flaked almonds
50g (1¾oz) apricot jam

*Sensational served warm with ice
cream, crème fraîche or cream with
a splash of amaretto stirred through.*

Pear and almond are natural bedfellows and the addition of citrusy, spiced ginger makes a winning ménage à trois. The basic frangipane recipe can be adapted to whatever fruit is in season – peaches, cherries, blackberries, apricots, plums…

Lightly grease and flour a 22cm (8½ inch) round, loose-bottomed tart tin. Place the flour in a large bowl, add the butter and rub in with your fingertips until the mixture resembles rough breadcrumbs. Stir in the icing sugar. Mix in the egg with a dinner knife to form a rough dough. Turn the dough out on a lightly floured work surface and pat into a disc. Wrap in clingfilm and place in the fridge for 30 minutes.

Meanwhile, make the frangipane. Place the butter and sugar in a free-standing mixer with a flat beater attachment, or use a large mixing bowl and a wooden spoon. Beat together until light and creamy. Slowly add the beaten eggs, in 3–4 stages, making sure that the egg is fully combined each time. Add the flour, ground almonds and almond extract. Fold in until combined. Transfer to a smaller bowl, cover with clingfilm and chill in the fridge.

Remove the pastry from the fridge. On a lightly floured surface, roll the pastry out to about 5cm (2 inches) larger than the prepared tin. Carefully drape the pastry over the tin. Press down gently to ensure the pastry covers the base and sides. Trim any excess with a knife. Prick the base all over with a fork and place in the fridge for a further 15 minutes.

Preheat the oven to 160°C fan/180°C/350°F/Gas Mark 4.

Remove the tin from the fridge and place on a baking sheet, line the pastry case with nonstick baking paper and fill with baking beans. Blind bake in the oven for 15 minutes, then remove the beans and return to the oven for a further 10 minutes to dry out. Allow to cool.

When the pastry case is cool, scatter the chopped ginger over the base. Top with the frangipane (this may need a quick stir) and spread it out in an even layer. Top with the pear quarters and scatter the flaked almonds over. Place the tart back on the baking tray and return to the oven for 45–50 minutes, or until the tart is golden and the frangipane has risen. Allow to cool a little on a wire rack, still in the tin.

Heat the apricot jam in a small saucepan on a low heat until loosened – add a little splash of water if it's really thick. When you're ready to serve, remove the tart from the tin carefully. Brush the jam over to glaze, then serve.

COOKING FOR A CROWD

The original idea for COOK was to do only meals for dinner parties, because inviting people over for a meal can turn into an almighty hassle. Inevitably, most of us get used to cooking for the number of people in our household. When we're confronted with additional numbers (and often a feeling that we need to impress), it can become a bit of a drama.

Here's what we've learned over the years about putting on a feast with the minimum of fuss.

KNOW YOUR LIMITS

The secret to feeding a crowd is to put in the work in advance – it really is all about the prep. If you don't have the time to invest up front, then don't feel you have to cook. Much better to get a takeaway or, of course, let us COOK for you. We regularly have customers call up and rather sheepishly request a recipe because one of their guests asked for it after dinner the night before. Now you can just pass on a recipe from this book. Done.

Once you're sure you've got time to cook, the question becomes whether or not to test the limits of your kitchen skills. A little foray into the COOK approach to personal development might help you decide.

At COOK, we talk about three zones of personal growth: comfort, stretch and scary. A comfort zone is a beautiful place but nothing ever grows there, as we like to say. To be comfortable all the time simply isn't very fulfilling or motivating. Nor do we want to spend too much time at the other end of the spectrum, in our scary zone – that's where high stress and burnout belong. So we try to have a good balance, with plenty of opportunities to stretch ourselves, occasionally going out on a limb, while also feeling relaxed and comfortable for much of the time.

While this approach is great for work (and life, generally), when it comes to cooking for a crowd, staying in our comfort zone is absolutely fine. Remember, the key to serving up joy is to enjoy the experience yourself! Recipes you're familiar with and confident about cooking are usually the way to go.

WHAT COUNTS AS A CROWD?

Like many things in life, this is relative. For a big family, there's a crowd to feed every mealtime. For others, a handful of people can seem like a hungry mob. So we're setting the bar low and defining a crowd as six people or more. This number stretches most of us beyond the ordinary routine. Eight plus often marks a special occasion. Double figures becomes a challenge. And once we're beyond twenty it's effectively mass catering.

WHAT ABOUT DIETS?

Make sure to ask what people don't eat when you do the inviting. There's nothing worse than having somebody arrive and say, 'Oh, you do know that Michael has gone paleo/keto/vegan/gluten free...?' If at all possible, you want a main course you can offer everybody – or at least a substantial side dish that caters to any special diets. What you don't want is to be cooking a little something on the side for just one of your guests.

HOW TO SERVE

For most of us, table space is limited, especially once you have glasses, candles, flowers, and so on, in situ. So figure out what will fit on the table for serving. While it's seductive to imagine bringing the main course triumphantly to the table to soak up applause from the crowd, it's usually much simpler to plate it up in the kitchen with just the sides on the table. Alternatively, laying everything out on a kitchen counter for people to help themselves is a lovely, relaxed way to serve, and means the table isn't overly cluttered. Plan what dishes you are going to serve from – dividing a side dish between two bowls, one at either end of the table, can often work well. Make sure you get all the plates, cutlery and glasses out before people arrive. Oh, and empty the dishwasher (if you have one), too.

DESIGNING THE MENU

If there's one golden rule for a stress-free and fun night as host, it's this: only have one element of the meal that needs your attention in the kitchen. In other words, you don't want to be actually 'cooking' while everybody is arriving or while they're sitting at the table – the hard work should all have been done in advance. You want to minimize time in the kitchen and maximize time with your guests.

WHAT MAIN TO SERVE?

The main dish tends to be the star of the show, so it makes sense to start here and build out. Think carefully before choosing. Anything that requires precise cooking is going to need lots of attention so, although it might end up being spectacular, you'll lose precious time with your guests. This is why we generally favour slow-cooked mains that are very forgiving when it comes to timings (and are easy to do in advance).

WHAT SIDES TO SERVE?

Think about colours and textures – you want contrast to keep things interesting. If you need to focus your attention on your main, make the sides as easy as possible. But if your main just requires decanting from a pot, you'll have more time for the side dishes. If you're feeding a veggie or vegan, maybe one of your sides could be substantial enough to be their main course? Salads are a great option, as they can be prepped in advance and dressed at the last moment.

For a larger crowd (well into double figures), we'd lean towards a big pot of buttered new potatoes or rice. Even more straightforward is simply to go with baskets of fresh bread (flatbreads, baguettes, rolls or sliced loaves from your local baker).

SHOULD I SERVE A STARTER?

We're a bit over the whole three-course thing, to be honest, at least in terms of spending lots of time making a starter. Some shop-bought nibbles (olives, crisps, dips) as we catch up over drinks does the job for us. If you want to serve something at the table, platters of charcuterie or smoked fish, with pickles and fresh bread, are a good option.

WHAT PUDDING TO SERVE?

The pudding should most definitely be made ahead of time. Try to make it a contrast to your main – follow a heavy main course with a lighter pudding, and vice versa. And don't overlook the no-fuss options. A big bowl of fresh fruit or berries with whipped cream or good-quality ice cream is always popular, as is a selection of cheese and biscuits.

WHAT ABOUT FINISHING TOUCHES?

Some simple table settings go a long way – tealights in old jam jars look great, as do a few fresh flowers if you have space. Don't worry about mismatched napkins, plates or glasses – it all adds to the charm. Use what you have available to add interest and visual appeal.

Don't forget sauces and garnishes – prep these in advance and make sure they're in bowls ready to go out on the table.

That's it. To get the ball rolling, we've included eight different styles of menu on the pages that follow, designed for different types of occasions. Always keep in mind that people have come to your house to spend time with you and your guests. Don't make it stressful for yourself. Don't be shy of asking someone to bring a side or a pudding. And, on the night, delegate where you can. Ask somebody to keep the drinks topped up; give the nibbles to someone else to hand round … and you'll know which guests are your best friends by whether or not they offer to help with the washing up!

Above all, remember that cooking for a crowd is all about serving up joy to everyone, yourself included.

MENUS

Slow-roast Joint and Salad

When your crowd isn't too big, slow-roasting a big joint (or two) is a great option – pop it into the oven hours ahead and forget about it! You can then take it out to rest and use the oven space for roasting potatoes or veg.

Serving is best done informally – shred the meat (which should fall apart) and remove the bones, mixing through whatever juices are in the pan. Either ask people to help themselves from the kitchen counter, or serve the meat onto plates and let people help themselves to the rest. Don't be afraid to mix things up with salads, roasted veg, flatbreads, roasties...

MAINS
- Slow-roasted Spiced Shoulder of Lamb with Mango Chutney (see page 145) **OR** Chilli, Ginger and Soy Slow-Roasted Pork Belly with Spicy Tomato Chutney (see page 87)

SIDES
- Parmentier potatoes (see page 138) **OR** roasted potatoes **OR** rice **OR** flatbreads (see page 36)
- Griddled Vegetable Minted Couscous (see page 165) **OR** Wild Rice Salad with Ginger and Lime Dressing (see page 166 – leave out the melon) **OR** chard or spinach sautéed with garlic **OR** Tenderstem broccoli

PUDDING
- Classic Lemon Cheesecake (see pages 195–6)

Wow! Push the Boat Out!

If you've got the time and want to stretch yourself, this is the menu for you. All of these mains are best for six people – you can double up if you have oven space, although you'll need to keep an eye on everything and potentially swap shelves around. While it's always tempting to carve/serve at the table, it introduces an unnecessary element of risk. You can always show off the complete item and then retreat to the kitchen to plate up (a bit like when they bring you a whole fish in a restaurant). Sides like dauphinoise potatoes and braised red cabbage can be cooked the day before and warmed up before the meal.

MAINS
- Salmon Rarebit with Roasted Grape, Walnut and Chicory Salad (see page 99) **OR** Salmon Wellington (see page 149) **OR** Rosemary and Sage Porchetta (see page 130) **OR** Beef Wellington (see pages 139–40) **OR** Huntsman's Chicken (see page 142)

SIDES
- Dauphinoise Potatoes (see page 183) **OR** roasted new potatoes **OR** Parmentier potatoes (see page 138)
- Braised Red Cabbage (see page 179) **OR** Cauliflower Cheese (see page 180) **OR** Creamed Spinach (see page 179) **OR** Tenderstem broccoli **OR** green beans

PUDDING
- Pear and Ginger Tart (see page 213)

Posh Barbecue

A barbecue has become the default choice for feeding a crowd in summer. To elevate it beyond burned sausages and burgers, make full use of your oven, too, and simply finish things over the flames. Put some effort into the salads – easily prepared ahead, dressed just before serving – and they'll steal the show.

MAINS
- Sticky Barbecue Ribs (see page 52) **AND/OR** Chicken Tikka Skewers with Lime and Coriander (see page 22) **AND/OR** Piri-piri Drumstick Traybake (page 55)

SIDES
- Griddled Vegetable Minted Couscous (see page 165) **AND/OR** Wild Rice Salad with Ginger and Lime Dressing (see page 166) **AND/OR** Lebanese-style Salad (see page 169) **AND/OR** Coleslaw with Toasted Halloumi (see page 170) **AND/OR** Roasted Harissa Squash Salad with Preserved Lemon and Apricot Dressing (see page 175) **AND/OR** Panzanella Salad with Crispy Capers and Croutons (see page 176) **AND/OR** a simple green salad
- Boiled new potatoes
- Plenty of fresh bread

PUDDING
- Vanilla Cheesecake (see page 195) – or one of the cheesecake variations

Laidback Entertaining

Invest in an extra-large pie dish (big enough for at least eight people) and prepare a lasagne or pie in advance that you can pop in the oven later on. It will keep warm, so is flexible for latecomers – this is a lovely, relaxed option.

MAINS
- Chicken, Ham and Leek Pie (see page 48) **OR** Lasagne al Forno (see page 56) **OR** Vegetable Lasagne (see page 60)

SIDES
- A big bowl of green salad
- Plenty of baguettes

PUDDING
- Chocolate and Pear Fondant Pudding (see page 206)

Moroccan-style Feast

This is our go-to option for ease and deliciousness. It can cater for most dietary requirements, there's plenty of variety to help make the table look spectacular, it works for any number and it's easy to prepare in advance.

For nibbles when people arrive, buy a selection of good-quality olives and dips like hummus and baba ghanoush. Serve with crackers or crisps and/or batons of raw carrot, pepper, cauliflower and cucumber.

MAINS
- Moroccan-Spiced Harissa Chicken (see page 25)
 OR Vegetable and Chickpea Tagine (see page 111)
 OR Moroccan-Spiced Lamb Tagine (see page 112)

For a small crowd, you can make the lamb tagine using shanks, one per person. Sear the shanks on all sides for 2–3 minutes until golden brown. Return to the pan after adding the chopped tomatoes, stock and chickpeas, with the bones pointing upwards, ensuring the meat is covered by the sauce.

SIDES
- Roasted Harissa Squash Salad with Preserved Lemon and Apricot Dressing (see page 175)
- Griddled Vegetable Minted Couscous (see page 165) **OR** simple, plain couscous **OR** rice (a more reliable option for a larger crowd)
- Carrot and Orange Salad (see page 112)
- Flatbreads (see page 36)

FINISHING TOUCHES
- Bowls of toasted flaked almonds, pomegranate seeds, chopped coriander, raita (see page 22) and hummus

PUDDING
- Gin and Tonic Semifreddo (see page 210)

Cook-ahead Casseroles

Cooking a casserole ahead of time is such a no-brainer. Not only does it make hosting stress-free but the flavours will deepen and the meat becomes more tender as it rests. Reheat on the hob over a low heat, adding a little water and stirring if the casserole looks like it's getting dry (adjust the seasoning if required). This frees up your oven space for something else (like dauphinoise potatoes or roasted veg).

Do be aware that making good, lump-free mash is tricky for large numbers, unless you use a ricer.

MAINS
- Beef Bourguignon (see page 84) **OR** Venison Casserole (see page 161) **OR** Coq au Vin (see page 100) **OR** Slow-Cooked Rump of Beef in Brandy (see page 133) **OR** Lamb Shanks with a Redcurrant and Rosemary Jus (see page 158 – although this recipe is space hungry, so you might only be able to feed 6–8 people)

SIDES
- Dauphinoise Potatoes (see page 183) **OR** mashed potato (add some horseradish if you're serving Beef Bourguignon) **OR** boiled new potatoes (serve with butter stirred through and chopped mint or parsley) **OR** roasted potatoes **OR** hasselback potatoes
- Creamed Spinach (see page 179), Braised Red Cabbage (see page 179) **OR** Cauliflower Cheese (see page 180 – this can double up as a vegetarian main) **OR** green beans

FINISHING TOUCHES
Using fresh parsley to garnish the main will give everything a lift.

PUDDING
- Raspberry Pavlova (see page 191)

Bowl Food for Many

When you've got a really big crowd (we're talking twenty plus), particularly outside the summer months, bowl food is the way to go. Big pots of pre-prepared stew or chilli, served in individual bowls, on top of a generous spoonful of rice.

MENU 1
- Chilli Con Carne **AND/OR** Chilli Con Veggie (see page 63)
- Rice
- Jacket potatoes
- Tortillas **OR** nachos
- A crunchy, green salad
- Bowls of guacamole, sour cream, chopped fresh coriander, sliced chillis and grated cheese

MENU 2
- Beef Bourguignon (see page 84)
- Rice
- Boiled new potatoes **OR** baguettes
- Green beans **OR** green salad
- Bowls of chopped parsley

MENU 3
- Moroccan-spiced Lamb Tagine (see page 112)
- Rice **OR** flatbreads (see page 36)
- Carrot and Orange Salad (see page 112)
- Bowls of chopped fresh coriander

PUDDING
Keep it simple with a big bowl of berries and cream or ice cream and/or cheese and biscuits.

Classic Buffet

It might sound a bit retro, but a big spread of cold dishes for people to pick and choose from always goes down a treat. Naming each dish on little blackboards or handwritten cards is a nice touch. For 12–15 people, we would suggest the following:

TWO BIG QUICHES OR TARTS
For example, Quiche Lorraine (see page 115), Roasted Red Pepper and Goats' Cheese Quiche (see page 116), French Onion Tart (see page 123) **OR** Caramelized Shallot, Celeriac and Stilton Tarte Tatin (see page 124).

TWO SUBSTANTIAL SALADS
For example, Roasted Harissa Squash Salad with Preserved Lemon and Apricot Dressing (see page 175) **AND** Panzanella Salad with Crispy Capers and Croutons (see page 176).

SIDES
- A simple green salad
- Boiled new potatoes
- Plenty of fresh bread
- A platter of cold meats and cheeses
- A variety of pickles and sauces

PUDDING
- A cheesecake (for example, Vanilla Cheesecake, see page 195, or one of the variations, or Baked Cheesecake, see page 199) **AND/OR** a rolled pavlova (for example, Cherry and Blackberry Pavlova, see page 190, Cinnamon and Autumn Fruit Pavlova, see page 191, Raspberry Pavlova, see page 191, Chocolate and Amaretti Pavlova, see page 189, or Fruit Vacherin, see page 200), with a big bowl of berries and some whipped cream.

INDEX

GLOSSARY OF UK/US TERMS

aubergine – eggplant
bacon lardons – matchsticks of slab bacon
baking paper – wax paper
beetroot – beet
butter beans – lima beans
caster sugar – superfine sugar
chicory – endive
chickpeas – garbanzo beans
chips – French fries
clingfilm – Saran wrap
coriander – cilantro

cornflour – cornstarch
courgette – zucchini
double cream – heavy cream
frying pan – skillet
gherkins – cornichons
green/red/yellow peppers – bell peppers
grill – broil/broiler
hob – stove
king prawn – jumbo shrimp
minced – ground
plain flour – all-purpose flour

prawn – shrimp
rocket – arugula
rump steak – sirloin
sieve – fine-mesh strainer
single cream – light cream
spring onions – green onions/scallions
sweetcorn – corn
tin foil – aluminium foil
tomato purée – tomato paste

GRATITUDE

If there's one free lunch in life, it's gratitude. Loads of research shows that expressing our gratitude to others not only makes them feel good, it raises our own sense of wellbeing, too. So, get ready for a love bomb...

They say it takes a village to raise a child and we've discovered it takes a fair-sized market town to make a cookbook. Mayor of our little town was definitely Claire Postans, brand director, who took charge of the project, oversaw the recipes and photography, tested many of the recipes (her neighbours ate well for months) and basically dragged everybody else over the finish line. Thank you. James Rutter, chief creative officer, conceived the book, wrote most of the words, did his fair share of recipe testing and made sure this is something we'll be proud of for years to come.

Hannah Goodacre, head of brand design, and designers Hannah Norton and Lily Summers all contributed to the beautiful look of the book (and the Hannahs helped with recipe testing, too). Mel Thomas was another recipe tester and also contributed the copy for A Freezer Full of Joy. Other eager home cooks who tested recipes were Mary Holmes, Jenny Tunbridge and John Wordsworth.

The original COOK cooks, Dale Penfold and Liz Dove, were hugely generous with their time, memories and recipe advice. Executive chef Jamie Wallace, the Robin to Dale's Batman and creator of so many iconic COOK dishes, was hugely supportive with his recipe knowledge, kitchen insight and expertise. The latest generation of development kitchen talent, George Wood and Joanne Gohil, were always available for feedback and ideas and pitched in with recipe testing too. Danni Brister at COOK Puddings was her usual helpful self. Robin Mcintosh was touchingly proud to model 'the claw' for us. Plenty of COOK chefs offered suggestions: Isie Akpan, Lee Austin, Jacob Barber, Chanaporn Beckley, Lee Birch, Darren Card, Victoria Croucher, Michael Ewens, Lewis Feaver, Marius Ghita, Ellis Hague, Chris Hosking, Orhan Houssein, Ricky Jantowski, Tony O'Brien, Reno Ruocco, Aaron Sleator, Louis Smith, Ashley Thorne and Aaron Walpole. Several shop team members also kindly sent in ideas: Angela Austin, Annabel Briggs, Peter Clarke, Tess McKeone and Emma Smith.

The wonderful Pip Spence occupied the third trimester of her pregnancy scaling down our big kitchen recipes to ones that work at home (welcome to the world, Audrey!). Sarah Vassallo tested them all out and was invaluable at our photoshoots.

For years, we've loved working with photographer Carolyn Barber and her stunning images for this book might just be her best yet. Thanks, too, to her husband Antonio and daughter Madeleine, who were on hand for impromptu modelling (not their first rodeo), as was Sarah Agyekum. Libby Silbermann looked after the styling and props and made sure everything looked absurdly delicious.

Sophie Perry gave over her beautiful home for our photoshoot and gathered together friends and family to eat: Kali and Elsie Hamilton-Stove, Melissa and Stephen Murdoch, Chris and Lucille Walker alongside the Perry clan: Andrew, Daisy, Ben, Daisy, Barnaby, Willoughby and Meg the dog. Susie Clegg did the props and Rosie French the food styling. Jenny and Rachel Perry kindly raided the family albums for photos, and Emilia Clapp was an ever-willing model.

The lovely team at Kyle Books remained reassuringly calm, patient and kind, committed to creating a genuinely beautiful book. Thank you, in particular, Joanna Copestick, Jaz Bahra (whose gorgeous children – Sahiba, Amreek and Asees – and almost-as-gorgeous husband Vik can be spotted in these pages), Leanne Bryan and Sarah Reece. The beautiful illustrations gracing these pages are the work of Holly Wales: thank you, we appreciate this definitely wasn't an easy gig!

We didn't know we needed an agent until we were introduced to the legendary Rosemary Scoular at United Artists. Thanks for taking us on (and to Allegra McEvedy for the intro and all her early advice and encouragement).

Of course, none of this would have got anywhere without the support, feedback and contributions of Ed Perry, Rosie Brown and James Perry. And then there's the rest of the glorious COOK community. This is for you. Without each other, we're nothing. Thank you for everything you do.